SALES JOURNEY

SALES JOURNEY

THE PROVEN SYSTEM TO MULTIPLY YOUR INCOME AND BUSINESS

MICHAEL TRACY

Published 2025 by Gildan Media LLC
aka G&D Media
www.GandDmedia.com

SALES JOURNEY. Copyright © 2025 by Michael Tracy. All rights reserved.

No part of this book may be used, reproduced or transmitted in any manner whatsoever, by any means (electronic, photocopying, recording, or otherwise), without the prior written permission of the author, except in the case of brief quotations embodied in critical articles and reviews. No liability is assumed with respect to the use of the information contained within. Although every precaution has been taken, the author and publisher assume no liability for errors or omissions. Neither is any liability assumed for damages resulting from the use of the information contained herein.

Front cover design by David Rheinhardt of Pyrographx

Interior design by Meghan Day Healey of Story Horse, LLC

Library of Congress Cataloging-in-Publication Data is available upon request

ISBN: 978-1-7225-0716-9

10 9 8 7 6 5 4 3 2 1

*This book is dedicated
to my wonderful and supportive wife, Tasha,
and my extraordinary and precocious children,
Romyn, River & Ryder,
who teach me new things about sales everyday.*

Contents

Preface 7
Introduction 11
1 The Sales Journey 21

Part One
Context

2 How Selling Has Evolved 31
3 Your Toolbox for Growth 35
4 Mind Control 71
5 The Sales Journey: How It Works 87
6 The Tree of Business Growth 91

Part Two
The Sales Process

7 Generating Leads 99
8 Prospecting 109

Contents

9 Qualifying Sales Prospects 131
10 Building Trust 147
11 Insight Selling: Why It's the Future 161
12 Discovery: The Art of Listening 175
13 Presentation: The Magic of Enthusiasm 179
14 The Close 197
15 Dealing with Objections 201
16 Multiple Sales and Referrals 207
17 Gaming the Sale 213

Conclusion 219
About the Author 223

Preface

ALL BOOKS ARE INFLUENCED by a combination of people and experiences. I can think back to a conversation I had with my father, the legendary motivational speaker and business consultant Brian Tracy, when I was young. He stopped what he was doing and walked over to sit beside me. With a serious expression on his face and piercing eye contact he said, "Michael, I have made a decision, and I don't think you will be happy with it right now. I have decided that you will inherit nothing from me, not a single dime." He paused for my reaction, then his expression lightened and he continued, "Instead, I will teach you how to sell, and Michael, if you know how to sell, you will never need to worry about money."

I was very confused because I was three years old at the time. You could say that was the beginning of my sales journey. Growing up, when I wanted something, I had to sell it: everything had to be positioned as a benefit to my parents. If I just stated that I really wanted something, I would never get it.

If I wanted a basketball, I would need to pitch it: "Mom, Dad, childhood obesity is increasing rapidly because the youth of my generation are becoming lazy and sedentary; they are occupied with video games, cartoons and potato chips. In fact, just twenty minutes of shooting hoops is the equivalent of walking for one hour. If I had a regulation basketball, I would receive enormous health benefits and would stay slim. In relation to the cost of the basketball, the replacement of my entire wardrobe to accommodate an increasingly larger and fatter body would be prohibitive." Then the close: "Can I have twenty dollars to buy a basketball?"

I was trained from a very early age to sell. That skill set has served me in sales endeavors and everything else. Sales is a collection of skills that provides a solid foundation to grow a business, accelerate a career, and have a better life. Now it is my great honor to share what I have learned with you.

This book is a labor of love. As I've discovered, most authors write because they are compelled by an inner voice that nags at them until they start writing. The same is true of this book: it's been a preoccupation of mine for several years. It also represents my experience in failing and eventually succeeding in a variety of industries, with different products and all types of prospects.

Anyone reading this book could toss it out the window right now and spend over ten years knocking doors, making calls, showing up to meetings in different cities and countries, delivering presentations, and closing sales. After about 10,000 hours, they will have discovered most of what you find in the pages ahead.

My intent is simple: to save you time. If you read and understand this book at the beginning of your career, I'm confident that you will save thousands of hours of trial and error learning time. If you are advanced in your career, I promise I will challenge your thinking and change your behaviors for the better.

That's my commitment to you: to pack this book with as much practical and actionable advice and guidance possible without boring you. I would be delighted to hear that after just a few pages, you jumped up and did something different that got you more and better results. After all, that's what this is all about: results.

Introduction

IN MY FIRST YEAR as a sales professional, I knocked on more than 20,000 doors and I got rejected almost 20,000 times. What sort of person would subject themselves to that sort of treatment? It's not as if I didn't have other options. I could have picked a safer job with lower income potential, but I didn't. Why?

The answer is that I didn't like the idea of putting a cap on my income potential. Having sales skills means that you have unlimited income potential, which is especially important in a society that equates money with success. Sales skills also jump you over the first stage of money making, exchanging your time for money, to the second stage: exchanging your results for money. In most other careers, it takes decades to make this transition. Now I'm older and wiser and realize that money isn't everything. But only people with money can say that, because if you don't have it, it's all you think about.

Although I was experiencing repeated rejection and failure, I started to make sales more and more frequently. My management team noticed, and I was offered a promotion to sales manager.

I was ecstatic, and I enthusiastically accepted. Only then did I inquire about my additional responsibilities. I was informed that I was now responsible for recruiting, training, mentoring, motivating, and supervising my own sales team. And I was to keep selling on top of all this: after all, my compensation was commission-only, with the addition of a small override on my team's production.

Without losing any enthusiasm, I went out and started recruiting people for the greatest job in the world: residential door-to-door sales! To my surprise, I learned that most people don't aspire to be door-to-door sales professionals.

I started targeting minimum wage employees at fast-food restaurants or gas stations and recent graduates (or nongraduates) from high school—essentially anyone who could walk and talk. I would sell them on the opportunity to make more than minimum wage—potentially a lot more. If they agreed, I would "process" them: do a light background check and generate an employee number. They would get a company polo shirt and a badge.

At this time, we were selling for a major US telecommunications company in Southern California's Inland Empire. New reps would attend in-office training three times per week and shadow me or an experienced sales rep before being set loose on their own.

Seventy percent of these recruits would quit in the first two weeks. The 30 percent who stuck it out longer went through an extraordinary transformation. This transformation is why I am writing this book, why I am proud to be in sales, and why I'm so motivated and enthusiastic about teaching sales skills.

In California at this time, minimum wage for forty hours a week was less than $200. Some of my recruits, after two weeks of sales training, went from earning $200 per week to $200 per day. That's a 500 percent increase in income in two weeks! Most of my team was composed of eighteen- to twenty-five-year-olds, with no college education and highly limited income potential. After two weeks, some were making more than their parents. After a few more weeks, everything about these new sales professionals changed: they started walking taller, wearing nicer clothes, reading books, and thinking about their future in a positive and expanded way.

Before, when these new reps presented themselves in the job market, the market judged that they were worth the minimum wage. Think about that: you go out to get employment, and employers are only willing to give you the absolute minimum. (I'm sure they would prefer to pay still less, but they are mandated by law to pay a minimum wage.) After a few weeks of sales training, the market changed its judgment: the new sales reps were now worth 500 percent more. As a direct result, their self-worth increased 500 percent as well. Their self-concept, their future potential, and their self-esteem all changed radically and positively. In less than thirty days, they had remade themselves into different people.

Repeatedly witnessing this transformation sparked my consistent and unquenchable interest in sales skills development, which I'm convinced can change the trajectory of a human life faster than any other professional skill set. I got very enthusiastic about sales training. I read more books, experimented with different strategies and tactics, attended workshops, sought out top producers to pick their brains, and became a dedicated student of the skill, art, and practice of selling.

During this time, I started my own marketing business, where I recruited and trained business-to-business (B2B) sales professionals. Then I helped build two large direct-selling companies, one of which surpassed 5,000 distributors worldwide. Afterward, I joined a small software startup as their head of sales and exploded their customer base by 1,000 percent in less than twenty-four months. That company was purchased by a large international bank, where I stayed on at the vice-presidential level for almost two years. After the team left the bank, we got back together and decided to start another software company, of which I became a cofounder.

My favorite part of every venture was an opportunity to develop people by teaching practical sales skills. That realization is why I started my business growth education company, Sales Journey, which is also the title of this book.

I started Sales Journey in 2017 because I got frustrated. I was in a constant hunt for more knowledge and applicable sales education. I got tired of hearing the "what" of sales and business growth. Here's an actual example from a workshop I attended. The speaker stated that to grow your sales and your business, you need to spend more time with qualified prospects, in fact, you should spend half your day with qualified prospects. I wrote it down, and when I looked around, I could see heads nodding in agreement. When I got back to my office, I went over my notes and read this golden piece of advice: "Spend more time with qualified prospects." I thought about it, then I said to myself, "Well, how the heck do I do that?"

That's when it occurred to me that very few sales trainers focus on tactics. Everyone focuses on principles and strategy, but rarely the tactical part or the how-to of sales.

The principles of sales haven't changed in over forty years, but all the tactics have changed, because the platforms are different. (I'll talk more about this evolution in chapter 2.) In 1980, you could go grab a phone book and "dial for dollars." Today I wouldn't know where to find a phone book and I'm pretty sure many of you reading this have never seen one. Today we have email, virtual meeting platforms, and messaging services too numerous to list. There are networks like Facebook (now Meta), TikTok, LinkedIn, Instagram, Twitter (now X), and YouTube, all of which use their own language and have their own taboos. There are new technologies like advanced CRMs (which is short for customer relationship management systems), automation, artificial intelligence, API (application programming interface) integrations, virtual reality, and more.

This book contains a collection of knowledge that is practical and universally applicable. It is for anyone whose sales results equal their income—which is everyone. Whether you know it or not, you are in sales.

Selling is a broad term that encompasses many different skills all working together in harmony. Here's a list of skills and traits I compiled that are required for sales success:

- Accept feedback
- Adaptability
- Attention
- Business ethics
- Coaching
- Collaboration
- Competitiveness
- Confidence
- Conflict management
- Conflict resolution
- Cooperation
- Courtesy
- Creativity
- Critical observation
- Critical thinking
- Customer service
- Deal making
- Dealing with difficult personalities
- Dealing with difficult situations
- Decision-making
- Dedication
- Delegation
- Dependability
- Desire to learn

- Dispute resolution
- Emotional intelligence
- Empathy
- Energy
- Enthusiasm
- Establishing interpersonal relationships
- Facilitating
- Flexibility
- Following direction
- Friendliness
- Giving clear feedback
- High energy
- Honesty
- Independence
- Influence
- Innovation
- Inspiration
- Intercultural competence
- Interpersonal skills
- Leadership
- Listening
- Logical thinking
- Management
- Managing difficult conversations
- Meeting deadlines
- Meeting management
- Mentoring
- Motivating
- Motivation
- Multitasking
- Negotiation
- Networking
- Nonverbal communication
- Organization
- Patience
- Perseverance
- Persistence
- Persuasion
- Planning
- Presentation
- Project management
- Problem-solving
- Proper business etiquette
- Public speaking
- Punctuality
- Reading body language
- Reliability
- Research
- Resilience
- Resolving issues
- Resourcefulness
- Respect
- Results orientation
- Respectability
- Scheduling
- Self-awareness
- Self-direction
- Self-monitoring

- Self-supervising
- Sense of humor
- Social skills
- Staying on task
- Storytelling
- Strategic planning
- Supervising
- Talent management
- Team building
- Team play
- Thinking outside the box
- Time management
- Tolerance of change and uncertainty
- Trainability
- Troubleshooting
- Valuing education
- Verbal communication
- Visual communication
- Willingness to learn
- Working well under pressure
- Work-life balance
- Writing reports and proposals
- Writing skills

This is also a list of soft skills that experts agree will be the most difficult to automate in the future. Which means that if you want a future-proof career path safe from robotics, AI, machine learning, and the Terminator, maybe it's as a sales professional.

What's that? You don't want to be a sales professional? OK, what about an entrepreneur, small business owner, lawyer, doctor, social influencer, video blogger, or solar installer? Sales skills are incredible all by themselves, but they're even more important when you combine them with another set of skills. Then you can make your career and your life potential explode.

Here's an example. Which lawyers make partner at big firms? Answer: the lawyers that bring in new clients. That's sales. If you don't want to make partner and prefer to hit your six-minute clock for billable hours forever, don't read this book.

What about doctors? Doctors don't need to sell, right? After you do your residency, the only way you make money as a doctor is by treating patients (= customers). So you can join a hospital system as an employee, or you can open your own office. Let's say you open your own office: how do you get patients? Answer: sales skills.

Startup CEOs spend a large portion of their time raising money, which is selling the future potential of their business to investors. They also need to sell the opportunity to talented employees and find customers for their products and services: all selling.

Solar installers can't install panels unless they have a paying customer—sales.

You won't get a job unless you convince a prospective employer that you are best suited for the job—again, sales.

We could go on.

Albert Einstein said, "Nothing happens until something moves." The corollary in business is: nothing happens until someone sells something. A sale is a trigger event. If we reverse-engineer the sale of a bar of soap, we can see how many moving pieces and how much activity are generated by a single sale.

1. Someone goes to the drugstore and buys a bar of soap.
2. A clerk rings up the soap, collects payment, bags it, and provides a receipt.
3. The clerk's job generates a paycheck, which she uses to buy a sandwich.
    - The sandwich shop makes the sandwich from ingredients on hand.
    - The sandwich shop's inventory of bread is depleted.
    - More bread is ordered.
    - Baker bakes bread.
    - Bread is loaded and delivered.
4. The store's inventory system is updated, generating a reorder to the soap distributor.

5. Reorder of soap is received.
6. Soap manufacturer accounts for new order in production.
7. Soap is packaged and shipped.
8. Shipper delivers.
9. Customer uses soap and smells nice, meets special someone, gets married, has baby, and so on.

All because a sale was made. Yes, this is an oversimplification, but the point is that no sales means no activity, and life as we know it stops. It's all very dramatic. The number one reason businesses fail is low or no sales.

You should read this book because you don't know what you don't know. A big part of selling in the twenty-first century is about your ability to understand and communicate insights with your potential prospects. The future of selling will be about adding value at every level, even before they receive your product or use your service.

1

The Sales Journey

There is a well-known formula for creating stories. It is known as the *hero's journey*, outlined by comparative mythologist Joseph Campbell and presented in his classic book *The Hero with a Thousand Faces*. The model was later adapted by Christopher Vogler as a practical guide for writing stories. The hero's journey also provided the structure for the plot of the Star Wars series, as discussed by director George Lucas in a 1999 film, *The Mythology of Star Wars*.

In this book, I'm adapting the hero's journey to personal and career development. I have modified this formula to reflect the reality of starting a business or pursuing a career in sales. However, this formula can apply to anyone who wants to make ongoing progress at almost any endeavor.

The first step in this time-tested formula is to understand where you are on the map on the next page. It is a matrix with four distinct sections: *mindset, action, leverage,* and *insight*.

SECTION ONE: MINDSET

This is represented in the upper right quadrant of the diagram.

1. **Your world,** symbolized by the globe at the top of the diagram. Everyone starts here when they begin something new. They are usually comfortable, maybe a bit complacent, in their current position. Although they enjoy the known routine of their work, they have a nagging feeling that they're not living up to their full potential.

2. **The call.** In this version of the hero's journey, the call takes place when, for example, your boss asks you to assume more sales responsibilities. Maybe you're a charismatic engineer who would better serve the company by working directly with prospective customers. Or you might be new and fresh out of college and you've been offered a position in sales, but you aren't sure you know how to sell.

3. **Refusal.** Whatever the circumstances, your first reaction is usually to refuse the call. This is the reaction most people have to change. Anything new is uncertain and disrupts your sense of security. Moreover, your self-limiting beliefs usually manifest at this point: "I'm not a people person," "I can't handle rejection," or "What will people think of me as a salesperson?"

4. **Inner work.** At this point, you must rewrite your mental programming. This involves understanding the responsibilities of your new position and getting used to the possibility of rejection, lost opportunities, and failure. You might read a book about sales or talk to someone who is doing it successfully as a way of warming up to the decisive moment where you cross the threshold and accept the position.

5. **The mentor.** Committing to your new position usually requires the aid of a mentor. The mentor can take the form of a book (like this one), a training course, or a person. The mentor provides the clarity and confidence you need to cross the threshold into the new world of sales.

SECTION TWO: ACTION

This section is represented in the lower right quadrant of the diagram.

1. **Fear and discomfort.** Now you're in the new world of sales. Picking up the phone scares you. What will you say? What if they don't like you? What if they tell you to go away? Oh no! You're uncomfortable: you don't have a routine or a comfort zone. You regret crossing the threshold, you'd like to go back, but it's too late. You need to stick it out. You need to be proactive instead of reactive.

2. **Tests and trials.** You feel the fear and do it anyway—picking up the phone, saying the wrong thing, trying again, and again, and again. Then something happens: you realize that rejection doesn't sting as much as the *idea* of rejection. You find new mentors that help you discover practical tactics that enable you to control the conversation and set up appointments. Eventually your manager starts letting you lead sales presentations.

3. **Allies and enemies.** You start making some sales and earn some valuable allies in your office. You make it onto the leaderboard, inevitably knocking someone else off. Some people start to resent your presence because your performance is making them look bad. You learn who wants you to succeed and who secretly or overtly wants you to fail. You offer to mentor new hires and let them shadow you.

4. **Irresistible challenge.** You are now skilled at the basics and are starting to see the potential (and commission) of landing a huge account. You develop a list with a few dream customers and methodically make inroads.

5. **Focused action.** You work late perfecting your presentation. You develop insights that will blow your prospects' minds. You engage multiple stakeholders, complete long requests for proposals (RFPs), and practice your delivery. You research your competition and even pretend to be someone else in order to hear their presentation. (In a movie, this would be the montage: an incredible amount of disciplined, focused work, summed up quickly with a peppy soundtrack and quick shots of you on the phone, writing things down, and doing presentations.)

SECTION THREE: LEVERAGE

This section is represented in the lower left quadrant of the diagram.

1. **The boon.** This is the *big win*! The boss personally pops the cork from the champagne bottle and pours you the first glass while patting you on the back; your colleagues are compelled to you give you high-fives when they pass you in the office. You landed the biggest client ever, and you're feeling pretty darn good!

2. **Boon leveraged.** High from your big win, your mentor comes into your office and tells you that now is no time to rest: now you'll need to work twice as hard. You're confused. "Now that we have the biggest account ever," your mentor explains, "we need to lever-

age that to get more big clients. We need to capture more market share, and we want you to lead the effort. Plus, all our competitors are going to see us as their main threat; they're going to make this an uphill battle." You follow your mentor's advice, and for several years your company grows, and you are well paid.

3. **Boon expires.** You do what you've always done, but it's not producing the same results. You're confident that you don't need to change: after all, you've spearheaded sales growth for years. It must be the market, the competition, the demand, and so on.

4. **Denial: final test.** It takes you a few months and a productive new sales hire to realize that you haven't changed your presentation for a long time, your insights are old, and your delivery is stale. It's *you*. Your skills need updating, you need to develop new prospects, and your style needs to adapt to the new realities of your market. You reluctantly conclude that you need to go to work on yourself.

SECTION FOUR: INSIGHT

This section is in the upper left quadrant of the diagram.

1. **Reflection.** You ask, what happened? Where did I go wrong? How do I recover from this slump? (And more introspective questions that force you to think and be objective.)

2. **Realization.** You realize that you're comfortable and you've embraced a routine. You're not changing, growing, or learning anymore. You are exactly where you started.

3. **Return.** You decide to retool, rethink, and restart your journey. You've mentored dozens of sales professionals; maybe it's time to manage them too. Or learn new skills, recreate your presentation, research, and learn new insights that you can teach to prospective customers. You develop yourself and get ready to continue your sales journey.

Now that you are familiar with the sales journey map, ask yourself where you are on your journey. Keep in mind that you may be on several journeys at the same time. For example, you could be leveraging your sales career to move to a position in management, finding a mentor, and then developing your management skills. Or you could be a successful entrepreneur who just sold their company. You can now leverage your unique insight and reputation to win over investors to fund for your next venture.

The point of the map is to help you identify where you should go next. You never want to get stuck in the same spot for too long. Resolve to identify where you are, then get moving, and stay moving. The goal is not to reach a destination, but to stay on your journey.

… Part One …

Context

2

How Selling Has Evolved

SALES, LIKE ALL PROFESSIONS, evolves and adapts to changing market conditions, economic trends, cultural priorities, and social taboos. In this chapter, I'm going to focus on the history of professional selling over the past half century.

The 1980s: Transactional Selling

The 1980s were a simpler time, and the profession of selling had yet to go through the fundamental changes that we'll discuss in the pages ahead. In those years, the phone was the tool of choice, wielded with precision and a collection of good closing techniques. Sales professionals could close deals, foster interest, get referrals and resales, and conduct almost their entire workflow with just a phone and fax machine.

This decade gave us the ABC of selling: *always be closing*. If you were in sales in the eighties and a potential customer had a question or a need for clarification, or if they needed pricing or delivery details, there was only one thing they could do: call you.

In this golden age, salespeople were the recipients of buying intent, so they could use the ABC method: always be closing. If someone called and asked, "Does it come in blue?" you could say, "Yes it does, but we only have one remaining in blue; what's your credit card number?" Or the customer could ask, "Can you deliver this by Thursday?" You could say, "Yes, we can deliver it on Thursday, but you would need to order it today. What's your credit card number?" The sales professional could start closing as soon as the conversation started. Each close would bring out a concern or objection, which could be answered, and then another close could be attempted.

You had quick-talking, fast-closing sales pros at car dealerships, banks, technology companies, and paper suppliers. If you were selling in the eighties and not closing all the time, you were leaving deals on the table. But something happened in 1994 that would change the game forever: the Internet entered the mainstream.

The 1990s: Solution Selling

In 1994, the Internet quickly grabbed a foothold, and the number of users exploded. Much like Johannes Gutenberg's printing press in the fifteenth century, which democratized book ownership and reading for everyone, the Internet democratized information, making practically all information available to everyone all the time.

This invention fundamentally changed the way people purchased products and services. The sales profession had to accommodate this new buying behavior. In 1995, if you had a question, "Does it come in blue?" you were typing that into AOL, Compu-

Serve, Ask Jeeves, or Yahoo. People stopped calling other people on the phone.

In short, the recipients of buying intent become giant search engines, and over time Google became the obvious winner. Being the best source of buying intent became Google's primary business model, and it still makes up more the 60 percent of its revenue. In fact, most of the other products Google developed have been created in defense of their search monopoly, such as Android, Chrome, Google Apps, and Gmail. Google currently pays Apple billions of dollars to be the default search engine on the iPhone, ensuring that buying intent still flows through Google.

Selling had to evolve, and it did. Consultative or solution selling methods allowed sales professionals to add value in a new way: they would ask great questions and listen intently as their prospect divulged their problems and pains. These methods are characterized by a discovery process, with lots of questions and a prolonged period of listening and verifying understanding. If you have ever been sucked into a sales conversation because you have been asked well-designed questions, you are familiar with these methods from a different perspective. We'll cover this process in detail in the chapters ahead.

Alas, times keep changing, and most people today recoil from the idea of spending time helping a salesperson discover pains and problems. In fact, the whole idea of spending any time doing anything is offensive. We have entered the hyperdistracted new world.

The 2000s: Insight Selling

Odds are that most people know their problems, pains, and needs. But now you go to Google to search your problem, and what comes back is 445 different potential solutions. If you are like most people, you stare at the options, find a review site, analyze the ratings and feedback from existing customers, and troll the message boards for some insight as to what solution to choose. Hours later, you burn out and decide that you can't possibly decide, because you don't have enough information. This is known as *paralysis through analysis* or *analysis paralysis*. The problem remains unsolved until a breaking point is reached, and the decision to purchase is made with a "screw it" mentality: "I'll just pick something and hope it works." This state of indecision makes purchasing decisions anxiety-ridden and off-putting. This is where insight selling makes a big difference.

In this context, the market is composed of all its participants, who either are or are not making buying decisions. Professional selling is aimed at making it easier for prospects to buy in any given market. In 1980, it was closing; in 1995, it was consulting. Today we use insight selling, which will be the prevailing sales methodology for the foreseeable future.

Insight selling is a branch or educational selling of education-based marketing. Simply, it is delivering mind-blowing insights that change the perspective of your prospect forever. Your ability to generate and deliver powerful insights will set you apart from your competition, create enormous reciprocity, and shave hours, days, or months from your sales cycle.

In the chapters ahead, I will thoroughly elaborate on how to do this.

3

Your Toolbox for Growth

THIS IS A LONG chapter, and for good reason. Your biggest differentiator in anything you do, including selling, will be yourself. You can't get more and better results without becoming more and better yourself. Every day, we must all be on a mission to be better than we were yesterday. This chapter will help you with a collection of tools, insights, and perspectives that will give you a solid foundation for career progress, goal achievement, task completion, and personal development.

The Triggers

If you've seen me speak, I frequently tell the story of my father teaching me how to swim by throwing me in the pool.

My father's generation, the preboomers, were young enough to remember the aftermath of World War II. They were teenagers during the Korean War and adults at the time of the Vietnam War. They didn't have patience for coddling and had no desire to insulate their kids from the realities of life. There were no awards just for participation.

In this case, there was the very real possibility of me drowning in the pool. As a parent today, I will tell you that I did not teach my children how to swim by throwing them in the pool. When faced with the very real possibility that they could wander out into the backyard and drown, my wife and I invested in a world-class pool fence and swimming lessons.

What does it feel like to get thrown into the pool without knowing how to swim? I'll tell you: it's shocking and mandates immediate action. In anticipation of being thrown in, your adrenalin starts pumping, activating your fight-or-flight response. In the water, you find yourself flailing and flopping around, contorting and stretching, desperately trying to keep your head above water. Your body fights by rapidly repeating different movements, using underdeveloped muscles you quickly (within seconds) figure out how to use to close the distance between your body and the edge of the pool. It's surprising how fast your body responds, learns, and gains competence—its only teacher being the new environment.

My father taught me how to swim and unknowingly taught me a powerful lesson that I have revisited my entire life: if I wanted to learn something new, I would have to radically change my environment. You can't learn how to swim by watching people swim or by reading books about swimming; you need to jump in and flail and flop, contort and stretch and repeat to succeed.

An extension of this lesson was the realization that I needed to be uncomfortable to grow, and in the absence of someone to make me uncomfortable, I needed to impose that discomfort upon myself: what I call "self-inflicted adversity." We live in an age of unprecedented affluence, comfort, and abundance. Each one of us needs to be ready to throw ourselves into situations that will force us to grow.

Two Mental Triggers

I created two mental triggers that I consider the bedrock of my personal and professional development. If you only learn and implement these two mental triggers, you will have paid for this book a thousand times.

MENTAL TRIGGER ONE

If you ever say to yourself, "That would make me feel uncomfortable," you must resolve to do that very thing.

As you get older, you will realize that comfort zones are not static circles: they shrink as you age. You also get better at rationalizing, even to yourself. The only way to stay young and nimble and grow is to beat back the barriers of your comfort zone by doing things and embracing opportunities that make you uncomfortable.

Everything worthwhile is going to be difficult. If it were easy, everyone would do it and reap the results. Consider it a test from the universe. The universe will always put two paths in front of you. One will be easy and comfortable; the other will difficult and uncomfortable. You must make it a daily habit to choose the inconvenient path—the difficult one.

MENTAL TRIGGER TWO

As you move down this path, you will notice your inner voice avoiding the word "uncomfortable," and instead the voice will say something like, "That would be really inconvenient."

Hence mental trigger two: if you are ever hesitant to do something because it's inconvenient, you must resolve to do that very thing.

You will not achieve anything worthwhile in your comfort zones, and opportunities to grow are never convenient. There are no successes of comfort or convenience. As my father would frequently say, "You can only coast in one direction." If you are prepared to set up these mental triggers, you will get enormous value from this book.

Your mindset, attitude, and way of thinking are the most important qualities you possess for personal and business success. In a knowledge economy, your highest-paid activity is thinking.

Thoughts Are Things

Thinking is a skill. The most valuable work you will do in your life will be thinking. The quality of your thinking will determine every aspect of your career, your personal life, your well-being, and every other facet of your existence. The French philosopher René Descartes said, "I think, therefore I am." Without getting too philosophical, your interpretation of what happens to you—that is, how you think—is your existence.

Thoughts are things. Every thought has a consequence. If you were to truly believe that every stray or rogue thought in your head would manifest in some very real way, would you be more careful about what you think? Yes, absolutely.

I am certain that every thought has a very real consequence. If you are not having the life you want, it's because you are not thinking correctly, or you are thinking about the wrong things. It starts there.

When I speak to groups large and small, I'll often ask the audience this question: "Look around. Can anyone here point to one thing that was not first a thought in someone's mind?" I'll give them a moment to ponder. To this day no one has ever discovered something that is not a product of thought. Now I'll admit I'm cheating a bit, because we're in a hotel ballroom or conference space, which is not a natural environment. But you can't get to a purely natural environment without the power of thought. Someone had to build a road or stomp out a path; how else would you get there?

Some people pick up a piece of fruit like an apple or orange and present it to refute the premise. Unless it's a wild apple tree and the apple fell by itself through a wormhole and appeared on the table in front of them, it's still a product of thought. Someone planted the tree, nurtured it until it bore fruit, picked the fruit, packaged it, and sent it off to market for sale. All of which required some serious thought.

If you entertain negative thoughts, negative things will happen to you. If you dwell upon anxieties, you will help manifest those very things. If you blame people, circumstances, or the environment for the present condition of your life, you will be unable to make progress in any direction.

The opposite is also true. If you fill your head with positive thoughts, positive things will happen to you. If you decide to accept people, they will accept you. If you think positively about changing the world and take action, you will make progress. If you want to marry a vegan yoga instructor, then become a vegan yoga junkie. You can have whatever you truly want if you're willing to be, act, and think about what you truly want all the time.

One of the first exercises you can do is to decide today that you are 100 percent responsible for your life, everything that has happened to you, and everything that will happen to you. I'm not asking you to accept fault for things that you can't control. Although they are not your fault, they are still your responsibility. You are still able to control your reactions to the things that will inevitably happen to you. If you can accept that for every great joy there will be a sorrow, for every pleasure a pain, for every happenstance of luck an equal and opposite misfortune, you will have developed your ability to respond: your response-ability.

When something happens to you that is not your fault, resist the temptation to blame. Instead say to yourself, "I am responsible" and repeat that phrase until you have repossessed your power. When you blame, you give your power away to someone or something else.

Your life and everything in it up to this point have been the products of your thinking. I need to spend some part of this book giving you practical tools to change your thinking so that you can stay positive and motivated and achieve your goals.

Critical Thinking

Your brain is incredible. It possesses an estimated 86 billion nerve cells, which are connected to each other in 100 trillion different ways. Imagine that: 100 trillion connections. Huge companies like Google, Amazon, Facebook, Open AI, IBM, and others are spending billions of dollars trying to create a computer with a capacity that could rival your brain: what they call artificial general intelligence (AGI).

If your brain were a piece of technology developed by one of these companies, it would be worth billions of dollars. AI (artificial intelligence) can only compile, reorganize, and regurgitate information that has already been created. Only your mind can produce novel and creative information and ideas.

Think about that! You're walking around with an incredibly powerful thinking machine. Just like with any computer, you need a fast, efficient operating system. If you're running an old, slow operating system, like Windows 95, you're not going to make much progress.

Unfortunately, you can't install a new operating system in your brain as you can on a computer. But you can learn some thinking skills. If you practice them over time, they will help you develop into a disciplined and efficient thinking machine.

Critical thinking starts with a decision to never again simply believe what you are told. Instead, you go to the source, read multiple viewpoints, be objective, and frequently challenge your own beliefs. The only way you are going to get an edge in life is through rigorous thinking. Western thought mandates us to be products of reason and trust our understanding over the noise of the consensus. In his book *Zero to One: Notes on Startups, or How to Build the Future*, Peter Thiel urges us not to compete but to create an entirely new industry or market, which we serve exclusively. The only way that happens is by critical thinking, challenging the status quo, and elevating our understanding beyond that of anyone else.

Because your brain is so powerful and you may not have been trained to program it, it does what it wants, and you are along for the ride. You are just a body for your brain to get what it wants: salty, sweet, and fatty foods; sleep; sex; dopamine hits; pain relief; and social connection.

To master your mind, you must focus on two areas. The first is thinking technique: maximizing the benefit of time spent thinking by having the right tools in your toolbox. The second area is thought control: using your mind instead of your mind using you. It's becoming a master over your stray and negative thoughts.

In sales, we are rejected all the time. We have setbacks; markets change; economies expand and contract. Our products and services are sometimes relevant and sometimes not. We need to use rigorous thinking to be adaptable.

A Short List of Fallacies

To start you on your journey, we need to expose you to some of your brain's favorite mistakes and lazy practices. This is not a complete list of every critical thinking fallacy. We'll touch on those that will have the most impact on your professional career and income.

FALLACY 1: CONFIRMATION BIAS

Confirmation bias is a pervasive little monster, causing us to misinterpret our world and believe things that aren't true. It starts when you decide to believe something; then your brain actively looks for anything that confirms the belief. It happens subconsciously, contorting and biasing your perception until you're convinced your belief is true.

Here's an example of one of my fallacious beliefs: "Everyone that drives a Toyota Prius drives slow and enjoys driving really slow in front of me." I go into the world with this belief in the propensity of Prius drivers to be slow. Because my brain is so powerful, it notices every slow Prius driver. This confirms my belief, and I begin to believe it with even more conviction. I might be at a dinner party and assert that if it were not for these slow Prius drivers, there would be less traffic. I might come to resent anyone who owns a Prius. Eventually, I'll end friendships and avoid people who own a Prius or just don't agree with my belief. Eventually, you'll find me living under a bridge without shoes and with no friends.

Avoid confirmation bias. Our brains will always find what they actively seek. Reposition the belief. Instead of looking only for confirmation, look for events that contradict your belief. Here's a better position to truly test whether your belief is true or not: I believe that all Prius drivers are slow, so I'm going to actively look for Prius drivers that drive fast. If you're looking for fast Prius drivers as well as slow Prius drivers, you will receive a much more balanced perspective, and you won't need to live under a bridge. (FYI, I still haven't seen many fast Prius drivers.)

FALLACY 2: HIGHLIGHTING AND DIMINISHING

This fallacy happens without our consciously realizing it. Highlighting happens when we receive information that both supports and refutes one of our beliefs. Instead of taking both sides into equal consideration and adopting a more moderate belief, we highlight the information or data that supports our belief, and we diminish the information or data that does not.

Take in new information in its entirety. If it conflicts with one your beliefs, don't resist; instead see it as an opportunity to expand your understanding.

FALLACY 3: BELIEVING WHAT WE ARE TOLD

Many people don't think rigorously about anything. They might regurgitate sound bites off the TV, assert a consensus opinion as fact, or be indifferent to or intolerant of other viewpoints. Most good thinkers know better than to engage in discourse with non-thinkers. It's like playing poker with a group that knows how to play poker versus playing with a group that does not. If you're playing with experienced players, you can play the cards, the people, and stacks according to the odds and your skill level. If you are playing with a group that doesn't really know how to play, none of your skill will matter, because everybody at the table is making erratic and nonsensical decisions. Don't listen to people who don't know how to think. And don't argue with them.

When someone tells you something that you want to believe, take the extra step to do some research on your own. Look for conflicting viewpoints and arguments before adopting this belief as true. There has never been more fallacious information in human history than there is now. AI, skewed algorithms, corporate bias, and the mainstream media are all in many respects working against the truth. The truth is your responsibility. It's a little extra work, but it's well worth the effort. You should regard new information as false until it's proven true, regardless of where it comes from. And it's your job to prove it true.

FALLACY 4: ACCEPTING THE MAP AS THE TERRITORY

The map is not the territory. Many of us—and I am no exception—have frequently adopted maps without examining the territory. I am referring to maps of thought: easy ways of thinking that mean we don't have to expend too much energy thinking for ourselves. We can go through our entire lives without understanding why we think and act a certain way.

If that doesn't terrify you, it should.

What maps are you using right now that no longer serve you, that are not accurate representations of the territory?

Do this exercise: sit and think about what maps you currently follow dogmatically, and ask yourself if you have ever glimpsed their basis. Sometimes you need to get off the map to see how warped it is. This happens frequently in business when a model that's worked extremely well for years stops working. This means the map no longer represents the territory and is no longer relevant.

Here's some business examples:

1. I had a friend, James, who was selling into Hewlett Packard (HP). He finally got a meeting with two high-level business developers whose mandate was to find ways to increase printable events. That's it! They wanted to know if my friend's service could help them deplete more ink cartridges faster. My friend explained that everything could be done on a smartphone, no paper or ink required. The HP people asked James if his company could tweak the service so that the user was required to print multiple pages. That's an old map.

2. Nokia, once the dominant mobile phone maker worldwide, watched as Apple's iPhone was released. They scoffed at the childlike interface and lack of keyboard. They stood still and watched Samsung, LG, Motorola, and others follow Apple's example. Nokia's mobile phone business slowly eroded into dust right in front of their faces. That's sticking to an old map. The same thing happened with BlackBerry: they watched it all happen and didn't change.

3. Blockbuster, once the dominant video rental company in North America, with around 8,000 locations, stood by and watched a little mail-order rental company come into the market. Blockbuster had the licensing agreements, the inventory, the supply chain, the logistics, and the staff to snuff Netflix out of existence. Netflix started with mail-order DVDs, then moved into today's streaming movies. In 2008, Blockbuster's then CEO Jim Keyes said, "Neither Redbox nor Netflix is even on the

radar screen in terms of competition." Blockbuster went bankrupt in 2011 and was then sold to DISH Network.

FALLACY 5: AD HOMINEM

Have you ever discounted an argument because you didn't like the person making it? Or instead of addressing an argument with facts and empirical evidence, you make your appeal based on the people and feelings involved? This is called the *ad hominem fallacy*, from the Latin for "against the person."

It's easy to find faults in other human beings and use those faults to discount legitimate positions, but you must resist this temptation, because it will entrench you into a dogmatic way of thinking. Annoying, amoral, and dishonest people can make good arguments that are worth thinking about objectively. Resist the urge to attack the person instead of the argument. If you want endless examples, just turn on any of the twenty-four-hour news station.

FALLACY 6: COMPARING YOURSELF TO OTHERS

The fastest way to lose your positive attitude is to see someone dumber than you make more money than you—or drive a nicer car, live in a nicer house, have more friends, or wear nicer clothes. I have news for you: there will always be someone who has more money, a bigger house, more friends than you. There will always be someone smarter, more charming, and more attractive than you.

The more you compare yourself with others, the more miserable you will become. Comparing yourself to others is a waste of time and energy that are better spent doing good work, expanding and challenging yourself, and growing as a human being.

On average, it takes about 10,000 hours to truly master any one skill. That's seven to ten years of focused work that requires you to face fears, frequently move outside your comfort zone, and work hard.

When you see people who have achieved great success, don't envy them. Respect their effort and get back to work. The fact is, everyone's story is different. You might be seeing the highlight reel on Instagram or TikTok, but you're not seeing the work, the failed relationships, the sacrifices, compromises, health issues, suffering, and misery behind the facade.

You want success? Get your own version of it, not someone else's. And you will get it if you do the work.

FALLACY 7: DESTINATION ORIENTATION

Destination orientation is the fallacy that you can reach a certain point in your life and then lie back: "As soon as I receive this promotion, I'll relax." "Just as soon as I finish this book, I can stop."

If you are old enough, you probably have suspected that there is no destination. If you have ever "arrived" at where you thought you could stop and relax, you know it was an illusion: just another milestone on this great journey that is life. If you decide today that you will never stop and you will keep going forever until you drop dead, your life will be better. Human beings are not meant to relax for too long. We're meant to struggle, and our life's meaning is a byproduct of that struggle. Our struggle is our story.

The Buddha asserted that all life is suffering. We suffer to reach a destination; once we arrive, we suffer more, because we know we can't stay. The only way to break this cycle is by becoming aware of it. If we know we're locked in a cycle of struggle and strife, we can enjoy the ride. We can be present to the good and bad without attachment or expectations. This is what Buddhism calls nonattachment.

The idea that there is a destination is poison for the mind. It inhibits us from making bigger commitments and taking on more responsibility as we get older. It stops us from stretching beyond our limitations. It stops us from our human mission: to add value and leave the world better than we found it.

FALLACY 8: PAST AND FUTURE ORIENTATION

How often do you think about the past? The future?

You can spend the better part of a day time-traveling into your past and future. There are very good reasons to think about the past: to glean insights from failures or successes, remember joys or sorrows, and analyze trends. Yet it's important not to get stuck in the past, wallowing in your regrets, mistakes, bad decisions, or sullied relationships.

The same is true when you think about the future, because it's totally unpredictable. When you spend too much time in the future, you may feel anxiety, stress, and worry. Plan for the future in detail, but be prepared for your plans to change frequently. Boxing legend Mike Tyson said, "Everyone has a plan until they get punched in the face." Tyson is describing what happens in life when you take action in any direction. No amount of planning can prepare you for that first unexpected punch in the face.

Spiritual teacher Eckhart Tolle exposes past and future thinking for what they are: a waste of the present moment. In his book *The Power of Now*, Tolle indicates that the only thing that takes us to the past or the future is our thinking. There is only ever one time, and that time is *now*.

If you think about this concept long enough, you will realize that Tolle is saying there is no past or future; what you think of as the past and future are simply illusions that your brain creates to distract you from the present moment. No amount of thinking can change your past, and no amount of thinking can accurately predict your future. The only control you have is making the right decisions right now. Your life is the product of your decisions, but you can't make them in the past or future.

The art of life is about making the right decisions in the present moment, and the right decisions are usually difficult. For example, if you wanted to lose weight, you would need to change your decisions daily. Doughnut or apple? Cheeseburger or chicken breast? Broccoli or potato chips? Your body is a product of your decisions right now; it's the cumulative outcome of what you decide in every moment.

FALLACY 9: THE CURSE OF KNOWLEDGE

The curse of knowledge is especially relevant if you're facilitating sales in any capacity. It is simply the mistake of assuming the person with whom you are communicating has the same level of understanding that you do.

Understanding is like a ratchet: once you understand something, you can't go back to ignorance. If you are oriented to imagine that most people are like you, which is normal, then you assume they also understand what you do. This can cause some very inefficient communication, lost opportunities, and lost revenue.

To combat this fallacy, come up with all the different elements that make up your level of understanding and list them out. Then attach a question that you can ask to verify the understanding of others.

Here's a short example: I've done consulting work for a large software development firm. They have two types of prospects: some are very technical, and others are more business-oriented. To find out which is which, I'll ask this question: what is the composition of your technology stack? A technology stack is the collection of programming languages, software, and services a company uses to support its products, web, and mobile applications. Depending on their answer, I'll choose what language to use and engage them at their current level of understanding. There is also the opportunity to elevate their understanding with insight selling (which I will get to later).

FALLACY 10: CORRELATION IS NOT CAUSATION

When something happens at the same time as something else, we naturally assume the two events are connected. It's easy to make a correlation and assume one has caused the other—in fact, it's too easy. As our default setting, it's important to see events as unrelated to each other.

Here's a quick example: my friend Chris asks to borrow my car, and I agree. Chris uses my car and gets a flat tire. The first assumption I could make is that Chris did something that popped my tire. But that's not fair. What if the tire was already pierced and Chris just happened to be driving it when it finally popped? Or what if Chris drove over a nail on the highway? Did Chris intend to drive over that nail? If I were driving, would the outcome be any different? Chris is a good friend and feels responsible. Should I make him pay the entire replacement cost for my tire?

At this time, it's important to realize that I don't have enough information to fault Chris or not. I must investigate further to find evidence and decide based on objective facts. Just because Chris was driving at the time my tire popped, it doesn't mean he was the cause.

Rules Are Not Laws

This thinking technique will enable you to act and maintain your momentum in the pursuit of your goals.

Another way to think about rules is to think about the games we like to play. Games are a collection of rules. The rules make games fun and engaging by artificially placing constraints on our behavior, which forces us to use economy, creativity, information, and skill to win. Everyone agrees, either directly or indirectly, to follow the rules before the game begins. When someone deliberately breaks a rule for their own advantage, we call that cheating.

But what if the rules are changed midgame? What if the rules are imposed upon you at random and without your knowledge? What if there are so many rules that nobody could ever possibly know them all, let alone follow them all? What if someone sees your progress and starts creating rules to limit your success or sabotage your mission?

This is what the game of life is like. There are countless rules and rule makers, all trying to exercise power over us. Sometimes we even create rules for ourselves based on our past experiences. We set limitations on our behavior. We establish boundaries we do not cross. We artificially create constraints that do not serve us or our goals.

We must make a distinction: some rules make clear sense, and others are complete nonsense.

What are nonsensical rules? Rules that can be broken without consequences. The only consequence could be someone pointing out that there was a rule that was broken. Or our own feelings of discomfort or inconvenience.

Good rules help organize our lives in a better and more effective way. Bad rules stifle and inhibit progress, particularly when they are followed blindly.

Many entrepreneurs use a philosophy called *first principles*. It advocates questioning to understand why something is the way it is. You must question every rule that holds you back from achieving your goal or mission.

Here are some first principles–inspired questions to help you discern good from bad rules:

- Why does that rule exist?
- Who made it a rule?
- Why did they make it a rule in the first place?
- Are their reasons for making the rule still valid?
- Did the rule maker have me or my situation in mind when the rule was created?
- Does it need to be followed?
- Most importantly, are there any consequences to breaking this rule?

If not, the rule may be broken.

Give yourself permission to break the rules. If a rule has no consequences, whether it's followed or not, it's a nonsensical rule and can be broken.

Think about Steve Jobs creating the first GUI (graphical user interface), iPod, and iPhone. Each time, he was told by establishment thinkers that there would be no demand for any of these products. The market had never seen these products before, so demand could not be measured. Steve Jobs' genius was to anticipate what people wanted and give it to them. This required breaking the traditional rules of business, that dictate a market be established before products are developed. Instead, Jobs introduced these novel products, and each product would go on to create its own market.

You've probably heard the expression, "It's easier to ask for forgiveness than for permission." Sometimes it's impossible to find the right person to ask. Often the rule is outdated, or, worse, nobody knows why it was created in the first place. If you stop and ask for permission for every bad rule that you encounter, you will be stifled at every turn.

Decide today that you have permission to break rules that don't make sense and have no consequences. Now you can maintain continual action in the direction of your goals.

Deep Thinking

As a culture we like the idea of making good decisions fast, but good decisions only come from slow and deliberate thought. In chess, the players must think many moves in advance, create contingency plans, and alternate maneuvers. The difficulty is holding all these things in mind at the moment it matters. In life, you must think about all the things that can happen as well as all possible responses so that when the time comes, you can make well-thought-out decisions.

To do this, you must train your brain to think deeply. How? It starts by scheduling time to think. Make an appointment with yourself; add it to your calendar. When the time comes, put away all distractions and write out a small prompt that you can repeat if your mind starts to wonder. Focus and think for at least twenty minutes. Write down any insights or ideas that come to you. Then level up: increase the time you allot to thinking and pick a more isolated setting with fewer distractions. You will find that thinking is like any other skill: the more you practice, the better you will become.

Allotting time to think will increase the quality of your decisions and elevate your performance above those who do not do this. We've heard the expression, "Work smarter, not harder." This is how you do that: by thinking.

Peter Drucker, the acclaimed management expert, made a distinction between efficiency and effectiveness; efficiency is doing things right, whereas effectiveness is doing the right things. In our lives, we will become efficient at the things we do repeatedly, and we will want to keep doing those things because we are good at them. Yet at some point, the skills in which we are most proficient will not be the skills we need to be most effective.

What things do you do efficiently? Are they still the most effective? Ask yourself these questions repeatedly to keep from falling into the efficiency trap: wasting hours, days, months, and years perfecting an antiquated skill set or practice.

Action Orientation

As you read this, the earth is rotating around its axis at a speed of 1,000 miles per hour. At the same moment, our planet is blazing an elliptical path around the sun at 67,000 miles per hour. As we swirl and spin around the sun, our solar system is hurtling through the galaxy at almost 500,000 miles per hour.

The point: everything is in motion all the time. Life is motion. Human beings have the unique ability to pilot their lives in this constant flux. We can think, decide, and act according to our own will, but we can only move in one direction, from the past to the future. Every decision we make and action we take determines our life's meaning. We can't stop the motion; we can only ride it.

Surfing is a good metaphor for life: you paddle out against the waves, fighting currents to get an ideal position. Then you start reading the waves as they arrive, and you constantly adjust your location between the swell and the break. Then the time comes when you turn away from the coming wave and you paddle as hard and as fast as you can. In a glorious demonstration of tidal energy, you feel propelled forward; then you pop up into a standing position to navigate away from the break and extend the ride. When the ride is over, you have an irresistible motivation to paddle back out and do it again.

In life at any given moment, some people are surfing, some are paddling out, and others are watching from the beach. Which one are you?

Action begets action. The more action you take, the more you do, the easier it gets to take more action and the more things happen—mostly good things. Decide to become a doer: someone who acts and gets things done. Resolve to be happy and content paddling out and doing the work. The best waves and longest rides are only available to those who are in position to ride them.

From the vantage point of the beach, you can imagine, extrapolate, and try to relate, but you will never truly understand. Are you spending too much time on the beach? Whole lives with unlimited potential can be wasted on the beaches of inaction. Grab your board, start paddling, and resolve never to stop. Become action-oriented and keep moving.

Gravity

We start our life in a weightless environment, warm, cozy, and ideally well nourished. Then we are born and thrown into earth's gravity, which plasters us down on the crib or floor. We can't raise our head, arms, or legs. It takes at least two years to get some semblance of balance in order to successfully resist gravity, stand, and walk.

As we get older and stronger, our bones lengthen and become denser. Now we can run, jump, ride a bike, and climb trees. As we move into middle age, we start to notice gravity's effects on our bodies. Our posture changes, our back hurts, our feet and ankles swell after a long day. As we age, our skeleton and muscular systems are warped by the constant, never yielding force of gravity.

Why is this a mindset principle? Because just like everything else on earth, we are subject to the elements and forces of nature. This perspective allows us to realize our impermanence and creates a sense of urgency to realize our potential and accomplish something meaningful with our lives.

Just as time only moves in one direction, gravity is working every moment, bearing the whole mass of the earth down on us. Weight lifters use gravity to strengthen their bodies. When you study weight lifting, you will find that everything is oriented around the straight line between the weight lifted and the center of the earth. All injuries happen when your joints are not lined up with that straight line. All progress depends on the successful use of gravity.

In the end, gravity will push you to the ground and help decompose your corporeal body. What you do before that happens is your decision.

Sleep

Sleep is essential to our mission of being productive human beings. It is how we transfer short-term memories into long-term memory. Without the requisite amount of sleep, we forget our experiences and lose pieces of ourselves.

If you have difficultly falling asleep, you're not alone. Sometimes we find ourselves rehashing the past, anxious about the future, or just thinking about all the things we need to do.

Before you fall asleep, make it a habit to write down everything you need to do for next day. Getting tasks out of your head and on paper is enough that you don't need to think about them while you fall asleep.

The latest research shows that a "complete sleep" consists of four cycles. Each cycle is approximately ninety minutes long. The deepest part of the cycle, which takes place at the end of the ninety minutes, is called REM (rapid eye movement) sleep. The fourth cycle is the deepest and most restorative. After each cycle, there is a brief period of light sleep that lasts approximately fifteen minutes.

If everything worked out perfectly, we would only need seven hours to attain four complete cycles of sleep. Alas, perfection is rare; hence the recommendation for eight hours of sleep per night. If we skip the last cycle, we lose a disproportionate number of sleep's benefits.

Avoid Distractions

This is the most distracting time to be alive. Never have there been more distractions, and never have they been more entertaining. The average middle-aged adult in the US spends almost 3.5 hours per day on a mobile screen. And it's not all in one sitting. It represents every distracting message, email, social post, and video that pulls you away from productive work time. In addition, the average adult spends almost four hours in front of the TV. That's 7.5 hours of every day spent consuming media and content: 47 percent of your waking hours. That is all input, no output. It is all consumption, no production.

Whatever you become or accomplish will be a direct result of your output or value contribution. If you are filling all your free hours consuming content of low or no value, it leaves very little time to create and produce something of value.

It's not your fault, but it is your responsibility. In defense of the distracted masses, there has never been more content available to consume. In the past, in order to create video content, you needed equipment, expertise, production, direction, distribution, and an audience. All these things are now accessible on the tiny device in your pocket.

At this writing, Amazon, Netflix, Apple, Google, HBO, CBS, Hulu, and others are investing heavily in original programming, releasing new shows and movies faster than any one person can consume them. We are in a renaissance of content creation, and each creation is its own distraction. In less than ten years, original shows debuting in the US increased 250 percent. In 2009, fewer than 200 original shows were released. In 2023, it was well over 516 original shows. That does not even include user-generated content: over four million videos are being watched on YouTube in any given minute. That is a ton of potential distraction. And be assured that all this information will soon be outdated, and there will likely be even more content.

To compound the problem, social networks compete ferociously for engagement. *Engagement* is the term they use to describe distracted people who scroll endlessly through their feed. In his book *Hooked: How to Build Habit-Forming Products*, Nir Eyal describes the mechanism that enables these networks to thrive. Eyal's goal is to help tech companies create habit-forming products. (In Silicon Valley, they refer to them as habit-forming, but any neurologist would call them addiction-forming.)

In order to make a product more addictive, developers provide a variable reward for using it. This habit-forming process relies on dopamine. Dopamine is the quick and addictive brain chemical released by our neurons when we drink alcohol, smoke cigarettes, eat chocolate, or do heroin or cocaine. It's the substance that causes and sustains addictive behavior.

Let me provide an example of a variable reward and the cycle of behavior it creates: When we walk into a casino to gamble, we start to receive a dopamine release. This increases when we sit down and put money into a slot machine, and it peaks when we pull the handle and the wheels start spinning. Humans get a huge dopamine hit when anticipating an unknowable benefit or variable reward. When the wheels stop spinning, our dopamine levels fall, whether we win or lose. So what do we do? We drop another coin into the slot.

Here is another example: We take a great photo of our dog and post it on Facebook. Throughout the next couple of days, we receive notifications—either subtle ones, like the red circle or numerical box floating over our mobile app icons, or audible notifications that pull us back into our Facebook (aka Meta) app. When we receive the notification, we get a hit of dopamine. An irresistible urge compels us to open the app and see what the notification is all about. We click, look, and find that someone has liked, commented on, or shared our photo. Our dopamine falls. After a couple days, the activity has stopped, and no one is commenting, liking, or sharing our dog photo anymore. So what do we do? We drop another coin in the slot by taking and posting another photo.

Think about it another way: have you ever really looked at your social media applications? Open TikTok, Facebook, Snapchat, Instagram, LinkedIn, Twitter (now X), NextDoor, or most others. You may be surprised to notice that they are all structured the same way. There is a place for media (photos, videos, etc.), some text, and three options: *like*, *comment*, and *share*. All the networks are identical in this regard. Why are they all identical? Because it works! Each social network has adopted the same habit-forming mechanism to increase engagement (that is, distract you more efficiently).

Billions of dollars are being spent targeting you, curating content that will keep you engaged, then selling your engagement to the highest bidder. This means you must be especially vigilant with your time and attention, because when you sell them to Facebook, you sell them cheap. As of this writing, Facebook's US ARPU (average revenue per user) is around $48 per year, or $4 a month. That's how much our attention is worth to them. *How much is it worth to you?*

Recent research has shown that it takes about seventeen minutes to recover from being distracted and return to focused work. If you are distracted by a text notification or email every twenty minutes, you will only get about nine minutes of focused work completed per hour.

Have you ever had the experience of being busy all day long, then you get home, sit down, and realize that you accomplished nothing? That's when you know you need more uninterrupted work time.

We live at a time that is witnessing rapid discoveries in neuroscience. The brain and how it functions are better understood today than at any other period in human history. It's your responsibility to learn how your brain works so that you can be less impulsive and more deliberate, becoming a better thinker.

Pen Power

A blurry image will come into focus when we adjust the aperture of a camera lens. A pen is like a lens for the mind: by using it, we can truly focus and capture the right ideas at the right time. Here are a couple of ways you can use a pen to increase the quality of your thinking:

Write it down. If you have an idea, write it down. The human brain can only hold one thought at one time. If you have a good idea and you don't write it down, you run the risk of losing it forever. As we've elaborated earlier, thinking is life; don't waste it. Often the act of writing down an idea will catalyze your mind and more ideas will flow from you. Keep a journal. History remembers those who write things down, because if *you* don't, *it* won't.

Read with a pen. When you read without a pen, you retain about 5 percent of what you read. When you use a pen the right way, you can retain over 90 percent of what you read. If you retained 90 percent of everything you have read, how much more knowledgeable would you be? Better equipped? More confident?

When you're reading, you're hunting for ideas and insights that will help increase your understanding. On this hunt, your pen is a spear. You should search through each page, discerning the most impactful points. Once found, they need to be skewered and brought back to camp. By underlining the point, you're identifying it. Once identified, you can think more deeply about it. This process of identification and thinking is like saving a file on a computer, enabling you to retain more.

Write a list. There are two types of lists: action lists and procedural lists. An action list is the classic "to-do" list, it lists the things that you need to complete. Try to keep these lists short, with 5 or fewer items listed per day. You can always add on if you complete all your items. If too many items are listed you will feel overwhelmed and may procrastinate. When you do something right and achieve a success, spend some time writing out what you did right as a procedure in linear order. Step 1, step 2, etc. Once you have refined your procedure, delegate it to someone else to see if they can duplicate your result. If they can, congratulations, you've just scaled yourself! This is the key to effective delegation.

Vocabulary

Increase your vocabulary. Words are the tools of thought. The average English-speaking adult has a vocabulary of around 25,000 words. The words we use every day are considered our active vocabulary. The words we rarely speak but understand are our passive vocabulary. It's estimated that Shakespeare had an active vocabulary of around 35,000 words and a passive vocabulary of an additional 30,000 words. That's a staggering 65,000 words!

The more words you know, the better and more precise your thinking will be. When you come across a word you do not know, circle it with your pen, then look it up. Think about how your new understanding of the word changes the meaning of what you are reading. When you stop discovering words you don't know, it's time to level up by reading more challenging books.

qOS

The human mind is like a computer in that it can be programmed. To program the human computer for achievement, we need to know how to program in the right language. Luckily for us humans, we can program ourselves using a very simple language: I call it qOS (question operating system).

Here are the elements of qOS:
- Why
- Who
- What
- How
- When

In that order. The *why* in qOS is a goal that you want to achieve; it's why you are going to go through all this effort in the first place.

The *who* is the people that you will need to help you as mentors, teachers, or connectors. Nobody can do anything meaningful all by themselves. You need to assemble a team of people to help you achieve your goal.

The *what* consists of all the cumulative actions that you will need to complete in order to achieve your goal.

The *how* is the process, system, or procedure you will use to accomplish the *what*. If it's been accomplished before, there is probably a method for doing it again.

The *when* is the schedule with deadlines: all the actions and procedures mapped over time. Time is a finite resource, and you must allocate it accordingly.
- Why = goal
- Who = mentors, teachers, connectors
- What = actions
- How = process, system, or procedure
- When = schedule with deadlines

Now make a list for each element, writing out each list in detail. When you are finished, execute and run the program.

Look at your goal. Call and connect with all the people on your *who* list, tell them about the goal you are trying to accomplish, and ask them for assistance or guidance.

Adjust your actions based on any new information, then execute the actions every day. Decide how much processing time you can allocate to your actions, but make sure it's at least thirty minutes every day, even on weekends and vacations.

Find a process, system, or procedure for completing your actions, optimize it, and write it down.

Refer to your schedule and deadlines every day. If you fall behind, allocate more processing time for your goal.

Commit to taking daily action on your goal. Schedule it on your calendar. Goal achievement is an incremental daily process. The goal achieved is simply the cumulative outcome of seemingly small and inconsequential actions completed consistently over time.

Time is the limiting factor for goal achievement. Since you have limited amounts of time remaining on earth (as we all do), you need to increase the value of the people you know, the productivity, effectiveness, and efficiency of the actions you take, and the systems you use.

The value of (who + what + how) needs to be greater than that of time. A time value that's higher than (who + what + how) indicates that your goal will require more time than you have remaining on earth. If the time value is higher than the value of (who + what + how), you'll need to make your goal multigenerational or find a young whippersnapper who can carry the torch after you're gone.

On the other hand, if you continue to meet people, refine your skills, and use better systems, you are increasing the value of (who + what + how) relative to the value of the time you have. You then may be able to accomplish your goal well before your inevitable demise and enjoy the benefits of a goal accomplished.

If you use qOS, you will notice accelerated efficiency gains as you meet new people, take action, and find better systems. You will be surprised how much you can accomplish in a short time.

Outcome Conundrum

If you have been exposed to any personal or professional development training, you know you can summarize most of it very simply: *goals*, *plans*, and *actions*. Every guru will tell you to figure out what you truly want, then make it a goal. Once you have a goal, you think it through and write out a plan of action. Then you do something every day that gets you closer to your desired outcome: your completed goal.

This is a good method, but it falls short because it neglects our neurological hard wiring. We humans have difficulty conceptualizing far-off, often abstract outcomes. In fact, the more we focus on the outcomes we want, the *less* able we are to make the right decisions daily. I have noticed repeatedly that many people don't really know what they want, and if they do, they do not understand why they want it.

This system will help you make incremental daily progress towards your desired outcomes. Moreover, by making progress, you will see how the outcomes you want today are limited by who you are right now.

I've built a system that transforms lives by translating outcomes into daily behavioral change. I call it my *decision program*. You start with your goals or your desired outcomes. Write down a goal for every category that is appropriate for your life. My categories are:

- Health
- Family
- Relationships
- Vocation or career
- Finance
- Spirituality
- Continual learning
- Personal growth

You can have as many categories as you would like, but don't choose too many, because this exercise might get onerous and you may not do it.

Now go through each category and write down a goal. When writing your goals, keep them *personal*, *present*, and *positive*. For example: "I earn $100,000 per month after expenses by June 1, 20XX."

"I" is *personal*.

"Earn" is in the *present* tense.

The goal is stated *positively*. A negative goal would be "I don't weigh 500 pounds by June 1, 20XX."

Be specific, make the goal measurable, and set a deadline.

"$100,000 per month after expenses" is specific. I can measure my progress every month until my goal is reached. "June 1, 20XX" is my deadline.

Once this list is completed, look at your goals. Next to each one, write down the decision and behavior that will be necessary to achieve it. Here is the list of the decisions and behaviors that I would need to engage in daily:

- Exercise (running, strength training, or yoga).
- Sleep (go to bed early and wake up early).
- Eat right.
- Work hard and in a focused manner.
- Finish tasks.
- Spend quality time with my wife and kids.
- Study and learn.

Once I have my list of daily decisions, I can translate this list into an affirmation:

I wake up early to exercise and read. I spend quality time with my wife and kids. I work in a focused manner on meaningful tasks that add value for my family. I eat healthy and nutritious foods. Every day I finish tasks that make a difference. I go to sleep early every night.

This is a good start. To keep myself accountable, I'll add specificity:

I wake up at 6 a.m. or earlier. I exercise by running or doing yoga or strength training for forty-five minutes or more. I read for one hour or more. I spend thirty minutes of quality interpersonal time with my wife and each of my three kids. I work in a focused and undistracted manner for six hours every day on challenging tasks that add value and contrib-

ute to the completion my goals. I eat organic vegetables, lean proteins, and heart-healthy fats for every meal. I am in bed by 10 p.m.

With this affirmative statement, I have relieved myself of thinking about abstract outcomes and refocused myself on my daily behavior. When I read this statement upon waking, I am enabling my goals to dictate my daily behavior. I am recommitting to that behavior every day. When I read this statement before I sleep, I will know immediately whether I have met, exceeded, or fallen short of my goals for that day. Every day, the program starts over. Every day, I am competing to be better than I was yesterday.

This is a foundational exercise for personal and professional growth. Do not wait. Do this exercise right now.

1. List your categories.
2. Write down one goal per category.
3. What would you have to do daily to achieve your goal? Write it down.
4. Create a list of behaviors based on your daily decisions
5. Create your affirmation statement.
6. Add specificity to your affirmation statement.
7. Read this statement when you wake and before bedtime every day.

By reading your affirmations (or eventually reciting them from memory), you will be overcoming cognitive dissonance. Cognitive dissonance occurs when your beliefs and actions are not aligned. By reciting your affirmations, you will be bringing them into alignment with your actions. At first, you may be able to go against your affirmations, but over time this will become more and more difficult. This exercise will force small, incremental behavioral changes that over time will improve every aspect of your life.

The Stages of Mastery

Nobody starts out good at anything. And nobody likes doing things they are not good at. So we have a chasm that needs to be crossed.

The first stage of any endeavor of mastery is the energy we get when something is new. The novel venture fosters curiosity and inspiration, pushing us into the next stage, which is beginner's enthusiasm.

When we start out learning something new, most of us can make it to the seventh or eighth week before we encounter our first humbling experience: when we realize we're not going to be at expert level without hundreds and thousands of additional hours of work.

With any new skill, it takes approximately eighteen months of hard work to successfully cross the chasm of competency. Once across this chasm, we become good at that skill and start to enjoy the endeavor. The enjoyment of competency creates a virtuous circle that propels us forward to mastery.

The second to last stage, reputational equity, is when we become known for being good at what we do. This is when people will seek us out, we'll get more referrals, we'll be able to charge higher fees, and people will ask us to mentor them.

Most people will not reach the eighteen-month mark or spend 3,000 hours acquiring a new skill. In fact 99 percent of people will quit long before their chasm is crossed. This is why so many CVs have short employment durations, especially with younger people. Now that you know what it will take to develop competency and eventual mastery, you can mentally prepare yourself with the fortitude necessary to persist until you cross your chasm.

Here are the stages of mastery, with the number of hours required cumulatively to achieve each stage:

1. Novelty: 100 hours
2. Beginner's enthusiasm: 250 hours
3. Humbling experience (chasm entered): 500 hours
4. Urge to quit: 1,000 hours
5. Light at the end of the tunnel: 2,000 hours
6. Chasm crossed: 3,000 hours
7. Competency achieved: 5,000 hours
8. Reputational equity: 8,000 hours
9. Mastery: 10,000 hours

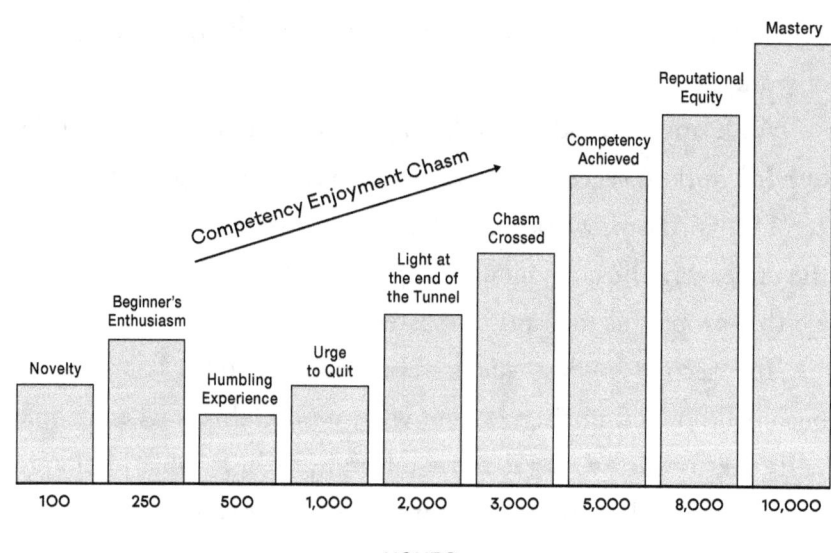

Mind Control

One way to manage your life is to think algorithmically. If you were a computer, this would be called machine learning: you analyze your daily actions and corresponding decisions, learn the pattern, and create an algorithmic response based on previous behavior.

The difference, obviously, is that we're humans and we can manipulate this process to achieve what we want. Instead of repeating old patterns, we can change our behavior one decision at a time. Each successful change replaces an old habit that is no longer serving us with a new one that makes us healthier and more productive.

Here's one way to utilize this approach. Take out a notepad and think about and write down all the decisions you make every day, from the time you wake up till the time you go to bed. Once this is completed, analyze your decisions and decide in advance which ones you need to make to achieve your goals.

When the relevant situations arise, remember what you decided beforehand and carry out the decisions you've already made. If the situation is common, routine, or predictable, make the best decisions in advance. You will find that deciding takes effort and consideration, but deciding in advance will make it easier to follow through.

Some of the most successful people wear the same clothes every day. Why? Because picking a new outfit every day can be a waste of time. Think about it: if it takes 5 minutes to dress in a predetermined outfit (your personalized uniform), it may take 20 minutes or more to select and put on a unique outfit. Furthermore, you need to add additional time for procuring new clothing items. Let's say the additional effort of wearing a modified outfit every day is 25 minutes versus 5 minutes for the time spent dressing in a predetermined outfit. That's an additional 20 minutes every day to get dressed. Multiplying this figure by 365 days in a year, you get 7,300 minutes—that is, nearly 122 hours or 15 full-time working days. That's more than two weeks that you can use for productive work, quality time with your family, or studying and learning. No wonder that the people who decide to wear the same thing every day are also some of the richest and most productive people in our society.

Managing Stress and Anxiety

The enormous gap between human evolution and technological innovation creates a variety of problems for us. Artificial lighting messes up our internal clocks and our sleeping patterns. The most abundant and inexpensive foods contain high amounts of fat, sugar, and salt. All of these were scarce during our evolution but, eaten in abundance now, have produced diabetes and obesity epidemics.

As primates, we became hyper anxious, which worked to our advantage at the time. In our evolutionary environment, our ancestors were not physically strong, so if we came across a lion, tiger, or bear, we'd be lunch. Humans evolved a heightened sense of awareness to compensate for our lack of physical prowess. Every noise, bush rustle, or branch crack might indicate a potential predator coming to eat us.

In modern society, mortal threats are far less common. Yet we need to live with our vestigial anxiety every day, and it causes many problems. Dealing with stress and anxiety tops the charts of psychological issues, and they are linked to physical maladies as well.

It's important to figure out how to manage stress and anxiety naturally. The tactics below are suggestions that have worked for me personally and for others. Please take what you can use and what makes sense for you.

1. **Mind, body, and soul represent one system.** When you're unified, you're at your best. Your mind and body are connected both physically and psychologically. Your brain thinks better when your body is healthy, and your body is healthy when you make good decisions about your life. You cannot separate the two without consequences. If you're feeling stress and anxiety, don't try to resolve it in your head; get out and resolve it with your body through exercise. If your body feels weak and lazy, decide to be strong and disciplined. One of the great revelations of psychology is that action proceeds feeling. Think about it: what would happen if you sat down and just waited for your body to feel strong and your mind to feel motivated? Answer: nothing.

To feel strong and motivated, you need to *act* strong and motivated. The more you "act as if," the more you feel the feelings you want, the more positive actions you take and the better you feel. This is a wonderful virtuous cycle, and you can take advantage of it at any time.

2. **Your inputs determine your output.** There's an expression in programming: "garbage in, garbage out" (often abbreviated as GIGO), meaning that you cannot get good output from bad input. If you have inaccurate numbers, it doesn't matter how wonderful your accounting reports look; they will be wrong. If you use bad syntax when you program, the result will be an unpleasant experience for the user.

In life it is no different. As an exercise, sit down and think about all your inputs: the things you read and watch, social media, the people you spend time with and talk to. Think about everything. What are you currently learning about right now? Are you exercising discipline and critical thinking? What inputs are holding you back from going to the next level? You should watch your inputs with as much discretion as the food you eat. This practice alone can have a significant impact on your life.

3. **Gratitude.** This is easily the most important mental orientation for relieving stress and anxiety and making you a more fulfilled person. Gratitude is thinking about all the things you have instead of all the things you *don't* have. The things you don't have are unlimited, that means the energy spent thinking about them is never-ending. It's a far better exercise to think about all the things you do have. It's about acknowledging all your unique advantages—talents, skills, friends, family, health, vitality, wisdom, and so on. According to the latest research, the outward expression of gratitude has the following benefits:
- Opens the door to more and better relationships
- Improves physical health
- Improves psychological health
- Enhances empathy and reduces aggression

- Improves quality of sleep
- Improves self-esteem
- Increases mental strength

If a pharmaceutical company created a drug that could deliver all the benefits of gratitude, it would be worth a trillion dollars.

The only way you can receive the benefits of gratitude is by expressing it, whether in writing, in person, over the phone, or through prayer. You must make your gratitude known.

In case you are still not convinced about the power of gratitude, I'll offer a powerful testimonial: almost every religion or spiritual philosophy incorporates a ritual practice of expressing gratitude. Why? Because it works.

Emotional Weather

People experience emotions differently. We all know someone who is whatever emotion they're feeling at that time. Unable to control their emotions, they surrender to them and let them control their lives. The other extreme consists of people who seem totally unemotional, whether from compartmentalization, an unwillingness to show their feelings, or lack of emotional intelligence.

Emotions are like weather: you can't control or predict them. They come and go, sometimes linger, changing spontaneously, using enormous amounts of energy or very little.

When you start seeing each emotional state as a temporary and fleeting condition, you can put distance between your thoughts and your emotions. This distance allows you to gain perspective.

Emotions can be very powerful tools, operating like a sixth sense. They can enhance your experiences, providing a rich layer in the mosaic of your perceptions. They can fuel your greatest endeavors. Often we act only when we get angry, excited, or inspired. I worked with a very talented entrepreneur who only started companies after he became angry. He would use the anger to boost his perception of an unaddressed problem and would create a company to solve it. The anger would be transmuted into a disciplined endurance while he waited for the market to catch up. The market's awareness of the problem would mature, and lo, the solution had already been developed. At that point, he would sell the company and find something else to get angry about.

Awareness of your emotions and how to use them can provide a much-needed edge in a highly competitive world. The converse is also true: tuning into the emotions of others will allow you to navigate relationships more tactfully, like a captain sailing a ship through stormy seas.

Thought Awareness

In any given day, you will be subject to thousands of thoughts, judgments, and rationalizations. Our brains are at work all the time, observing, filtering, and interpreting the world around us.

The way you feel is dictated by the thoughts you entertain. When you dwell on positive thoughts, you will feel more hopeful and motivated. When you dwell on negative thoughts, you will feel more fearful and less motivated. The human brain is really that simple.

If you're reading this, it means that you possess above average intelligence. This in turn means that you are likely to be skeptical of the belief that the thoughts you entertain could really impact your entire life. It may seem too simplistic as an explanation, but often the simplest explanations are correct.

Here is a great exercise to bring some awareness to your thinking: set a timer to go off every hour. When the timer's alarm sounds, write down exactly what you are thinking at that very moment, with no censorship: you can always burn the evidence later. After a couple of days, go back through and circle all your positive thoughts with a blue pen and all your negative thoughts with a red pen. What type of thought dominates? Positive or negative?

A positive thought is hopeful. It assumes that the world is a good place and so are the people in it. A positive thought assumes the future will be better than the present and that most people are inherently good and moral.

A negative thought is based on fear. It assumes that the world is a bad place and so are the people in it. A negative thought assumes that the future will be worse than the present and that most people are inherently dishonest and possess evil intent.

If you have more than 50 percent positive thoughts, congratulations! If your thoughts are more than 50 percent negative, you have some serious work to do. More positive thoughts equal forward momentum: progress in the right direction. More negative thoughts mean regression: no progress. That means all you need to do is make sure more than 51 percent of your thoughts are positive. Once this is achieved, you can step on the accelerator: more positive thoughts equal faster progression. The results of this exercise alone will be astounding.

Here is a dramatization of positive versus negative thinking. Ask yourself: whom would you want to be around in this scenario?

You wake up in the morning.

Positive. Wow! I woke up, I'm alive. Today is going to be amazing!

Negative. Fudge! Another day! I'm going to be late, I hate my job. This sucks!

You get caught in traffic.

Positive. Excellent! More time to listen to my audiobook.

Negative. Arrgh! Screw this! Just *go!*

You arrive at work.

Positive. It's so great to have a job at the best time in human history to be alive! I wonder how much of my paycheck I can save this month.

Negative. What a bunch of jerks! I need to figure out how to look busy so I don't get fired. What's the point of all this BS?

You're asked to work through lunch to hit a deadline.

Positive. A challenge! Bring it on! I've got more mental endurance than anyone here and I'll prove it. Plus, replacing lunch with a few peanut butter pretzels will help me lose weight.

Negative. Are you joking! I'm not getting any more money, so why should I spend any more time? I hate my life.

You get home and there is nothing in the fridge.

Positive. Perfect! I felt like tacos anyway. I'll plug into my audiobook and walk to Roberto's.

Negative. Damn! Looks like cereal for dinner. This day could not get any worse.

You receive a call from your mom.

Positive. Love . . . So happy to hear from her. How is she doing?

Negative. I don't have time for this. I want to binge on my Netflix. What does she want anyway?

Each one of these thoughts, positive or negative, is a choice. Your thoughts dictate who you are, but you are not your thoughts. You can choose to change the way you think and what your internal monologue will be. Every thought has a consequence, and the combination of all those consequences is your life.

Think of it this way: when you're talking to yourself in your own mind, who's listening? A part of you, commonly called the *subconscious mind*, listens and accepts everything you say as true. It never talks back; it just goes to work to manifest the things you think about and say to yourself, positive or negative.

Thought Substitution

How do you change your thinking? The answer is simple. Earlier we noted that your mind can only hold one thought at a time. To control your thinking, you must first become aware of the thoughts you are paying attention to. When you notice that you are dwelling on something negative, you simply need to substitute it with something positive. Once the positive thought has been loaded, the negative thought will die of neglect. If you do this enough, you can fundamentally change how you interpret the world around you.

A huge plus is that the more positively you think, the more you flush out the negative people from your life. The best way to annoy negative people is to be positive, proactive, and hopeful: it drives them crazy.

Decisions

The most powerful force on this earth is the human ability to decide and execute. When you evaluate the world around you and your current situation with right thinking, you can make decisions that are designed to better your future and which you execute by taking massive action.

Some people are not where they want to be right now simply because they have failed to make the right decisions at the right time. Or, worse, they failed to decide at all.

In sales, most objections are rooted in a reluctance to decide. A decision is a powerful act that represents a commitment and a risk. Whether you're making a buying decision or a lifestyle decision, your ability to decide and execute will determine your future.

How do you make good decisions? I use a simple system that I will share with you. In the matrix below, you will see four types of decisions. The first type of decision is a *bad/dumb* decision as represented on the lower left quadrant. The second type is a *bad/smart* decision in the upper left. Third is a *good/dumb* decision in the lower right. The best type is the *good/smart* decision in the upper right. In this context, good and bad refer to morality.

Bad/dumb decisions are morally wrong and have a high probability of negative consequences. Robbing a store for money is a great example. The robber might get away with it but will likely get arrested and end up in jail.

Bad/smart decisions are morally wrong, but the negative consequences are not immediate. For example, if someone lies on their college application, they might get into college and start a promising career, but their whole life could end up in scandal if this fact is discovered later in life. Another example: if someone sells something that they know is defective, they will make a sale and some commission, but the reputational damage, compounded over time, will leave them struggling to convince others they are trustworthy, stifling their progress.

Good/dumb decisions are morally sound, but the consequences don't serve long-term goals. For example, someone donates half of every paycheck to a church. This is a good thing morally, but consequently this person has no savings and eventually loses their home. Or someone cashes out their retirement early and goes on an epic vacation. It's a lot of fun, but now they're broke.

Good/smart decisions are both morally sound and serve a long-term goal. You should strive to have all your decisions plotted in this quadrant. Examples are saving for your future, sacrificing some fun to study and get into a good college, finding good friends who support and encourage you, exercising regularly, and forgoing unhealthy foods.

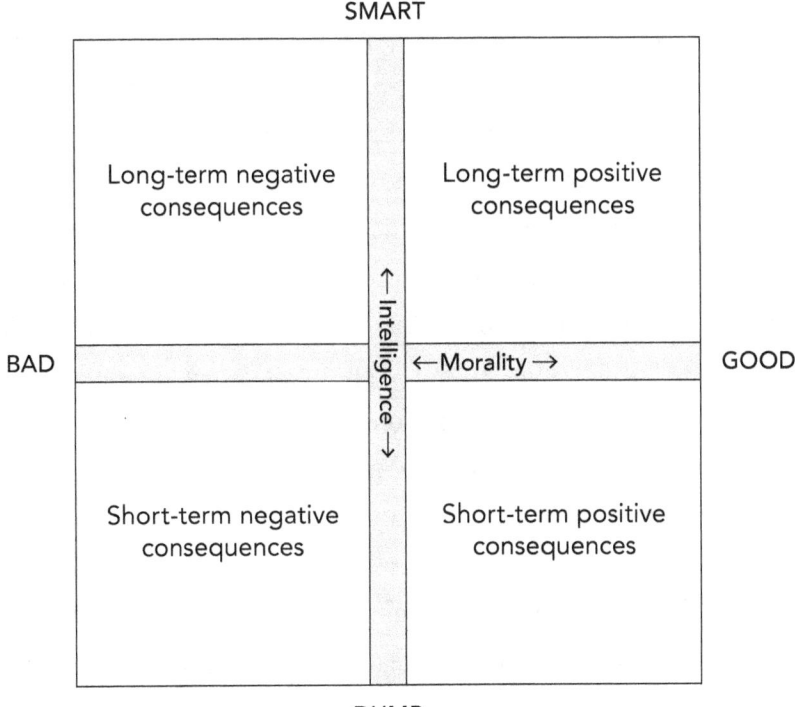

Write down all the decisions you typically make in a given week. Think about everything: what time do you wake up? Exercise? What did you eat? Did you stay in your comfort zone, or did you force yourself out? What did you do last weekend? What have you decided to do this weekend?

Once you have a good list, get into the practice of plotting your decisions on this matrix. Pay attention to where your decisions are being plotted. If you are making too many bad or dumb decisions, endeavor to make more good and smart ones.

Change Your Mind

Now that you have some tools to make better decisions, it's important to have one more: the power to change your mind. Yes, decisions are commitments that we make to ourselves to adjust the trajectory of our lives. Yes, we should take our decisions very seriously. After all, if we can't keep the commitments we make to ourselves, how can we be trusted when we make them to others?

But on some occasions, we decide on and execute a course of action and then realize that we are not happy or that we are moving in the wrong direction. When this happens, we must quickly reevaluate our decisions and, if necessary, change our mind.

In business, there is a common expression: "hire slow, fire fast." This means making the decision to hire slowly and thoughtfully, but when we notice it's not working, we move quickly to terminate the employee.

Think of every decision you make as a new hire: is the new decision adding value to your life or diminishing you in some way? As soon as you notice that a decision is now a problem, act quickly to fire that decision from your life.

The power to change our mind is a liberating force. Compounding a bad decision by delaying a change or correction can lead to more bad decisions and unnecessary compromises. When you have made a mistake, you should embrace it, learn from it, and take quick corrective action—in short, change your mind.

The Responsibility Paradox

I have discovered a paradox in life, and it is counterintuitive. When I explain it, many do not accept it. Possibly it's a relative truth: it's true for me, but not for everyone. With that said, once it is explained, you will intuitively know if it's also true for you.

I have found that as I get older, I need to accept more responsibility and make bigger commitments to feel fulfilled. Every human starts life with zero responsibilities. A baby is totally dependent when born. If we extrapolate the natural progression of a person's capacity for responsibility, it becomes apparent that responsibility and its corresponding commitments must increase over time.

To simplify, there are two types of people. The first type seeks to be happy through absolute freedom from responsibility and commitments. This type of person feels responsibilities as handcuffs or anchors weighing them down. Something as small as a scheduled appointment might haunt them for days or weeks before: they see it as an assault on their absolute freedom. Any commitment may as well be a prison, dictating where they can go and when. Becoming reliable is an affront to their desired state of absolute freedom.

The other type, of whom I am part, are the responsible, committed, and reliable types. A well-known device called the circle of responsibility depicts a series of concentric circles surrounding any one person. The first level is self-responsibility: being responsible for your own life. The second circle is your family. The third, your friends. The fourth, your community. The fifth, your society or country. The sixth, your environment, and so on.

As you get older, you start to expand into new circles of responsibility. When we are young, we focus on self-mastery, controlling our impulses, developing discipline, and honoring our commitments. When we are ready, we commit to a partner, then to a family. Each commitment represents more responsibility and more sacrifice of freedom. We come to realize that absolute freedom is illusory, and the pursuit of it is childish—childish in the sense that children do not know any better. Once we know the joys and fulfilment of being committed and responsible, it's impossible to derive joy from a life without their fruits.

Similarly, entrepreneurs that create a business and become committed to its success assume a great deal of responsibility. The owner of a company feels responsible for each employee and their families. Owners see themselves and their company as extensions of their own family. The neuropsychology of entrepreneurs and parents is strikingly similar.

The other fascinating phenomenon that happens when we accept more and more responsibility is that we are compelled to rise to the occasion. We expand past our previous limitations and become better, stronger, smarter, and more resilient. We begin to see responsibility and commitment as signposts pointing the way to our future potential.

Microfailures

Rejection, mistakes, and setbacks are the best teachers. The only way to succeed in business in general and selling specifically is to learn, try, fail, optimize, and try again. This cycle produces a highly refined source of direct market feedback. Direct market feedback is gold and oxygen for any business. Salespeople are on the bleeding edge of revenue generation, and you need to be in close quarters to get bloodied.

Each selling interaction that results in a rejection is a small lesson. Some rejections have taught me when to ask a certain question, highlight a particular benefit, or abstain from a direct pitch. Over time, these microfailures helped to refine my pitch, rate of speech, tone, posture, facial expression, and distance. There is not a person on the planet that could have taught me these lessons faster than this process of trial and error.

Each subsequent job or business was the same. We grow in the direction of resistance. No resistance = no growth. If it's easy, we are either a master or a fool; and if we are unsure which, then we are the fool.

Rejection and failure are necessary for acceptance and success. Just like day versus night, cold versus hot. You need one to have the other. If you spend your whole life minimizing rejection, you will not make much progress. Rejection avoidance will kill not only your business and sales goals but your ability to find a partner, get a promotion, and pursue your dreams. My father advised me in my formative years that to have a high rate of success, I would need to have a higher rate of failure.

Selling is the art of maximizing positive outcomes in a sea of highly erratic and variable interests. To navigate this sea, you need to know whom to target, how to engage your prospects, what language to use, and how to position your business. Most importantly, you need to be courageous and enthusiastic in the face of repeated rejection.

The Sales Journey: How It Works

THE SALES JOURNEY METHODOLOGY is a holistic approach to sales, marketing, and business growth. For sales, it outlines a tested process that will inform all your activities and business goals. Without a functional and flexible process, you would be relying on your impulses and intuition, which will only occasionally yield the results you want. Without a process, your results will be inconsistent and not duplicable.

You can use the elements of this process to build your sales system. Here is each stage of the process:

1. Lead generation: finding common and creative ways to consistently generate leads.
2. Prospecting your leads and converting them from names and numbers into real opportunities.
3. Qualification: making sure the prospect has the need, desire, and ability to pay for your products and services.
4. Establishing trust and rapport. Are you credible? Do you have experience? Who else is happy with your product or service?

5. Discovery. This is when we ask good questions and find out how or if we can deliver real value.
6. Presentation. How do we teach, inform, and persuade people to make a buying decision?
7. Closing the sale: finalizing the business and converting a prospect into a customer.
8. Handling objections, compromising, negotiating, and demonstrating that we're experts.
9. Resales and referrals. Let's get our customers to buy again and tell their friends so that we can build a sustainable business!

As my father once told me, "Michael, nobody ever starts out good at anything." Plenty of talented people are broke and destitute because they failed to refine their craft; they lacked the discipline to develop the core skills necessary to fully leverage their natural talent.

The wonderful thing about sales is that all the requisite skills are learnable. You do not need to be talented; you only need to be yourself. In this book and in my sales training program, I use the following key terms:

Skills. Abilities that you will learn, apply, and improve over time.

Tools. Assets that you will begin to develop as you read this book. The assets that you develop will need to be refined and optimized in the marketplace. Your tools will be forged in the fire of iteration and action.

Mindset. These are ways to stay motivated, energetic, and enthusiastic. You will also learn how to utilize your mind to become sharper, quicker, and more competent.

Insight. New perspectives and information that will increase your understanding of the core concepts.

Action. Exercises that you will need to perform to truly internalize a lesson. Once you know and act on something you learn, you own it forever.

Action is the most important lesson you can learn from this book. No matter how much time you spend reading, understanding, and thinking, if you do not try to do something, you're wasting your time. After all, there are no prospects in this book, there are no sales here; everything you seek is out there right now.

Please follow this instruction throughout this book: if something causes you to pause and get inspired, put down the book and try it. Make a phone call, go to a networking group, create a post. *Do something!*

Action begets action, and every action starts something moving, setting off a chain reaction that builds upon previous actions, ultimately culminating in success or failure. Take more positive actions: add value, elevate the understanding of others, contribute even when there is no obvious benefit, and wonderful things will start happening for you.

6

Tree of Business Growth

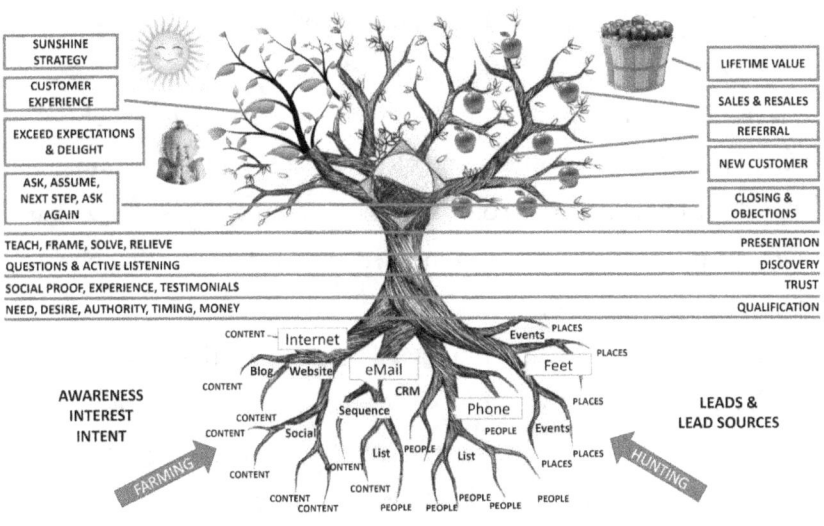

IMAGINE THAT YOUR BUSINESS is like a tree. Trees have roots, a trunk, branches, leaves, and fruit. Every business's tree is a little different, but they all follow a similar template. The business growth tree in the example pictured is an apple tree.

The sustainability of any business depends on consistent and reliable leads. Lead generation is the most important part of the sales process. In fact, without leads, there *is* no sales process. On your tree of business growth, your root system is your lead generation strategy.

The root system of the tree is composed of five large roots that branch open at the ends into smaller roots, like blood vessels and capillaries. The five main roots are *Internet, social media, inner circle, contacts,* and *feet*.

The Internet root is your website, blog, press releases, features, stories, and anything else that someone can find by searching for your business.

The social media root is composed of every network on which you have an account, including TikTok, Facebook, Instagram, LinkedIn, YouTube, NextDoor, and Yelp!

Your inner circle is composed of the people who know, love, and trust you. These are your parents, friends from high school or college, your wife, brothers and sisters and their spouses (maybe). This is the collection of people who truly want the best for you and your family. They want you to succeed and will do almost anything in their power to make sure you do if you ask.

The next root is your contacts. These are all the people whose numbers you have stored on your phone. These are people with whom you have already had some interpersonal contact. They will remember you if you call them and would not recoil at hearing your voice.

The last root is your feet. Your feet are remarkable, because they can take you places. Your feet can walk you to your car and press the pedals to get you anywhere you need to go: networking groups, workshops, business meetings, conferences. Your feet can also drive you to the airport and take you anywhere in the world if the occasion calls for it. Your feet are so important for your sales success and business growth goals because the most powerful way to connect with another human being is to meet them face to face, eye to eye, and belly to belly. You simply cannot reach your potential as a sales professional or business owner unless you are willing to move yourself into situations where you can make meaningful human contact.

These five roots together represent your ability to attract, cultivate, collect, organize, and pursue leads for your business. In the diagram, you can see that the Internet and social media roots are on the left side of your tree. The central, and deepest, root is your inner circle. Contacts and feet are located on the right.

The positioning of these roots is deliberate. The roots on the left side of your tree are marketing roots. Think of the left side as your "farming" side. To farm successfully, we must plow the field, till the soil, plant the seeds, keep the soil moist with water, control pests and blights, trim, and finally reap the harvest. This is not something anyone can do in a day or week, or even a month. Farming is a daily contribution of time and energy with no guarantee of results. A cold spell might destroy the crops before they bear fruit. This is a risk you need to take.

The inner circle root is the first root that enables your tree to grow. This root provides support in many ways, and most are not money related. Before you can start a business or embark on a commission-based sales career, often you need to have a good support structure. Your inner circle can provide mentorship, encouragement, and support when times get tough. Often your inner circle will be your first source of leads and introductions. If you are starting your own business, your inner circle will likely be the source of your first investor.

On the right, you have your contacts and your feet. You can reach out to your contacts at any time; after all, they are only a phone call away. You don't need to sell each contact you have stored in your phone; just tell them what you are doing. Tell them what you are selling and who would find it valuable. The more people that know what you are doing, what you are selling, and understand the value it provides, the better. You can cast a wide net quickly just by getting the word out. You might be surprised how much business you get and how many deals you close just by reaching out to people you already know and empowering them to refer business to you.

Your feet can take you places, and the more places you go, the more you expose unknown unknowns. Often we start our careers and business with lots of erroneous assumptions. When we go out into the world and explain our products and services for the first time, we're often surprised when our prospects don't understand what we are saying. Or worse, they understand what we are saying but show little interest. It forces us to reevaluate our messaging and our engagement strategy. Sometimes we need to reevaluate our entire business model. The best business teachers are other well-informed businesspeople, and you will have to go out and find them to refine your craft.

It may surprise you that the roots on your business growth tree don't need water to grow. These roots are different. On the left side of the tree, your Internet and social roots need content to grow. These roots have an insatiable need for more and better content. Content that's interesting, surprising, and entertaining must be added consistently to your website, blog, and social networks to attract the right prospects.

Your inner circle root needs lots of attention. Positive, undivided, quality attention is the only thing the inner circle root wants; feed it.

The contacts root does best when it's organized and updated. Make sure to use some system to keep your contacts fresh. Sometimes a simple spreadsheet will suffice. Unless your memory is perfect, I would suggest some sort of CRM, or customer relationship management solution. (I'll use the term *database* instead of CRM sometimes. Please note that they're synonymous.)

Your feet need places to go: events, conferences, meetings, workshops, networking groups. Make sure to feed this root as often as possible.

Part Two

The Sales Process

In part two, we will elaborate on the sales process and describe both strategic and tactical approaches to each category. The goal of every business is to create and keep customers. To create a customer, a business must develop a product or service that solves a problem, fulfills a need, relieves a pain, or helps overcome a current challenge.

For a prospect to choose to buy your product or service, you will need to understand that prospect as well as or better than they understand themselves. There is a specific collection of skills and tools that will enable you to do this.

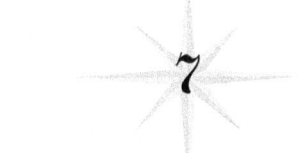

Generating Leads

For every business, there are four focal points that will determine success:

1. The ability to generate leads consistently and cost-effectively
2. Delivery of your promised product or service in a timely and efficient way
3. Creating a customer experience that generates delightful experiences for your customers
4. Cultivating and maintaining high levels of trust

In this chapter, we will focus on the first element: sales leads. They are the blood and oxygen of any business. Without a consistent source of leads, your sales growth will be variable and sporadic.

What is a lead? A lead is a contact that may need and want your product or service. They may not know your company exists or that your products and services can help them. They may well be ignorant of your value proposition. It's even more likely that they do not truly understand how your product or service can solve their problems, relieve their pains, and overcome their challenges.

Leads must be approached from their own perspective and level of understanding. They have no patience to listen, read, or educate themselves about what you have to offer. They are concerned with their own needs: how to serve their own customers better and more efficiently, how to reduce their costs, and increase their profits and the quality of their products, services, or lives.

Because of this preoccupation, leads are considered cold until meaningful contact is made. When you reach out to a lead, your mission is to convert them from lead to prospect. If it's the wrong time, you can put them in the freezer (for possible contact later) or eliminate them entirely to refocus on other leads.

To simplify, a lead is simply a name, number, and email address—and often less than that. Having reliable lead sources and efficient ways of converting those leads into real prospects is essential to a thriving business.

How can you consistently generate good leads? Whole books have been written about lead generation. Just as every business is different, every lead generation strategy needs to be customized for maximum effectiveness.

The options are numerous. For online businesses, a good lead might be an email address. For a car dealership, it's a person walking onto their lot. For a pizza place, it might be everyone in the neighborhood surrounding their business.

It's best to reverse-engineer your lead generation strategy by using a successful sale as a blueprint. For simplicity, let's say you own a pizza restaurant. A successful transaction happens only three ways: someone walks in and orders a pizza to go; someone walks in, orders a pizza, and eats at the restaurant; or someone calls in and orders a pizza for pickup or delivery. In this example, you only need two things to happen: someone walks in or someone calls in. How do you get people to behave in this way? Now it gets more complicated. Here is a partial list:

1. **Signage.** People need to see your business and like your sign. This also creates multiple impressions when they drive or walk by. This means your location is very important.

2. **Product quality.** The pizza must taste good. It doesn't matter how many people you get to walk or call in: if the pizza isn't super delicious, you will not receive repeat business.

3. **Price.** There are usually many options for pizza, so you don't want to lose because you charge too much. With that said, if you're using organic ingredients imported from Italy and specially designed clay wood-fired ovens, you may be able to charge a premium.

4. **Service.** If you make any hungry person wait too long, you will lose business. Your service must be prompt, speedy, and responsive. The faster your service, the higher the perceived value and the more important your customers will feel.

5. **Social proof.** People feel more comfortable doing what other people are doing and buying what others are buying: it reduces the perceived risk of making a mistake. Having a line out your door is the best advertising money *can't* buy. For the same reason, you never put out an empty tip jar: you need to seed it with cash to make customers more comfortable tipping. Some of the most successful restaurant launches give away their food on their first day to create buzz, a long line, and positive reciprocity.

How many ways can a prospect buy from you? In person, over the phone, online, and so on. Each path needs to be defined, and on each one you must ensure the prospect receives the right information, education, and motivation to make a purchasing decision.

As an exercise, write down every way a prospect can purchase your product or service. Then detail each step. Interview your existing customers and ask them why they chose your business over the alternatives and competitors. Use that information to optimize and grow your business. Every customer you currently have is a treasure of information you can use this way. When was the last time you interviewed one of your current customers?

Build a Lead Machine

As mentioned earlier, a business needs a reliable and consistent source of leads, which are crucial for your business success. A consistent source of leads will allow you to scale up faster, because consistent leads often make it possible to hire a sales professional. If you are a sales professional, you know that the quality of the leads you receive makes a huge difference in your ability to close new business.

The marketing department is usually tasked with generating consistent leads. The leads are then passed on to the sales department to follow up and close new business. The most frequent problem in this relationship is a lack of communication between marketing and sales. Marketing campaigns are frequently created to produce a specific outcome: more leads. When campaigns capture interest that is unrelated to the product or service being sold, it will stifle sales. You can imagine how this plays out: the marketing department blames the sales department for not closing the leads they provided, the sales department blames marketing for providing crappy leads, and on and on it goes.

This conflict is cancerous to business growth. Everyone in your organization should be 100 percent focused on the customer. If the marketing department truly understands the problems, pains, and challenges of existing customers, they can hammer those hot buttons with every marketing campaign. As a result, the leads they pass on to sales will be red-hot, and the sales teams will be ecstatic. Morale will explode, and so will your company.

I've worked with many entrepreneurs who start companies. Inevitably they get stuck attempting to generate enough leads consistently. They make mistakes, and once they have a consistent lead generation machine, they decide not to build the business at all but instead to sell the leads to established businesses doing the same thing.

The point: generating leads is a business unto itself. Generating enough qualified leads for your business is a special skill set which determines whether your business grows or fails.

A lead machine converts money into leads. For example, Google or Facebook advertising is where you input money, and the output is a varying number and quality of leads. The quality of these leads will be determined by your targeting criteria, marketing messages, and capture incentive.

Targeting criteria are demographics like age range, gender, income, interests, and location. You can save a lot of money by achieving clarity on your targeting criteria. It's easy to spend too much money too fast by being unspecific about even one attribute.

The key is to put enough money into your campaign to validate it and confirm that it will drive the traffic you need to generate the leads you want. Once it's working, you can allocate more money to it, knowing the results you will receive. Don't make the mistake of spending too much on your first campaign. Unless you're a seasoned Internet marketing professional, spend small amounts of money. Validate and iterate to achieve success.

Next, you must master the message. You may know there is a need and desire for your products, but if your advertising messages don't effectively communicate what problems you solve and what pains you relieve, no one will choose your business. The sad truth is that mediocre products and services often sell more because they are better marketed, with clear messages and compelling copy.

For every minute you think about your brand and your message, you will save $100 and one hour of your time. You must get this right.

Do whatever it takes to validate your marketing messages. Hire an expert copywriter; conduct micro campaigns; ask colleagues and counterparts to provide honest feedback. Take your ego out of it. This exercise will pay dividends when it matters most. Test everything before you commit a sizable budget.

Also consider the opportunity cost. Sometimes we're so focused on one method that we neglect to consider other, more effective ones.

Finally, what incentive will you provide to capture the lead? You've done all this work iterating a lead engine that's driving traffic and keeping that traffic engaged with good marketing messages. Now you need to capture the lead before they move on, click on something else, or keep scrolling. You must offer something they absolutely need and only give it to them after they have completed a contact form, called you, or formalized their interest in some other real way.

The most common method is to create a lead magnet. A lead magnet is a compelling piece of content, a sample, trial membership, or free item. The only requirement for receiving this lead magnet is that the prospect provides accurate contact information. You can ask for a first name, last name, email, phone number, address, number of employees, yearly revenue, and many other things. But just know that the more information you require, the fewer leads you will capture.

The industry standard is an email address. You deliver your lead magnet to the prospect's email upon submission. This validates that the email you received is real and not made up.

Cultivate a Lead Field

Your lead strategy also requires a field. A field is something you nurture over time. Just like a farmer, you must till the soil: keep your website and social profiles current and relevant. Plant the seeds: develop insightful content and an editorial calendar that's consistent with your brand and overall marketing strategy. Water the seeds regularly: post the content on the appropriate social networks and on your website's blog. Prune your crop by engaging with every comment and reciprocating "likes" when you receive them.

Your field will require consistent time and energy every day, so allot a period of time to maintain this strategy. It doesn't work in spurts and sprints. It's only effective as a daily activity.

The result of a well-developed and growing field will be your harvest: leads. The leads will trickle and flow depending on the economic or industry environment. When developing content, spend most of your time on content that doesn't expire, commonly referred to as "evergreen" content: something you write and post today that will live on the Internet forever. When your content is insightful, interesting, and thought-provoking, it becomes a magnet for attention. This content will draw in new leads long after you have forgotten about it. You will eventually have the cumulative effect of hundreds of pieces of content, then thousands. All this content will draw attention to your company and your products.

There are countless examples of good blogs becoming businesses. In this new world of sales and marketing, the content can precede the business. Are you thinking about starting a business? Instead of investing money into developing a product or service, choosing a location, or doing market research, try starting a blog about the problem you're trying to solve. Create interesting content, and see if you get any engagement. Ideas can be validated quickly with little investment if you can refine your skill at creating good content.

Dig a Well

Everyone possesses a wonderful source of leads that's instantly accessible: the phone in your pocket. The average adult has 500 contacts stored on their phone. These are 500 people who know you. Some actually like you, and a few love and adore you.

When I explain this source of leads to my trainees and students, many recoil at the thought of calling someone they know socially and attempt to sell them something. This is a common misunderstanding. I would never advise anyone to sell things to their friends and family—unless you don't like spending time with your friends and family.

Utilizing your stored contacts to enhance your sales and business growth requires a specific strategy that does not involve you selling anything. When you call someone you know, instead of selling, simply explain your business, whom you serve, and the results you deliver. Then ask this question: "Is there anyone you know that may benefit from a conversation with me?" If they do, great! Ask for a short email introduction. If they do not, don't worry: you have just planted a valuable seed that has made someone that knows and trusts you aware of the problems you solve, whom you serve, and the results you deliver. This increased awareness will start to manifest in more introductions, referrals, and invitations.

If the people who know you, trust you, like you, and love you don't know what you are doing, how can they help you? And everyone needs help. Nobody can do anything meaningful or significant by themselves.

8

Prospecting

LET ME TELL YOU a story about a gentleman I met named John. John had been successful at his last company. He met or exceeded his quota every quarter for three years before deciding to move on to higher-priced enterprise solutions. He discovered a new startup company and was quickly hired. His managers trained him on the product and gave him access to the CRM. John logged in and, to his surprise, found no leads assigned to him. He inquired about new leads. His boss told him that they didn't have a marketing department and John would need to prospect his own leads.

John's heart dropped, and a feeling of heavy dread came over him. At his previous company, the marketing department was well developed, and John could count on at least five or ten new leads per day. All he had to do was click a lead and start an automated contact sequence, which most of the time would result in a confirmed appointment. Then he would just run the prospect through the presentation that was prepared by management. This approach would usually allow him to close 30 percent of the leads he was assigned. Now John looked at the empty list of prospects in his CRM like a dark void in space.

What could John do? Where would he start? Expectations on his performance were high, so for the first time in a long time, he felt fear and anxiety.

I met John at one of my workshops, and he had a flurry of questions. He described his situation, and I gave him some guidance, which I will give you. I told him to start small: just find five new people every day. Go on the Internet, Linkedin, or other free databases. Find some names, the right titles at the right target companies. Google the email syntax for that company. Plug the emails into an email verification utility (of which there are several online). Call, voicemail, and email every new contact with the explicit goal of scheduling a short call or virtual meeting. In your messaging, focus on the results that your product or service delivers, not on the features.

John left that day empowered and we stayed in contact. His results were not instant: it took almost three weeks for him start getting good appointments. He increased his prospects from five per day to ten, then to fifteen. He set up his own prewritten responses and started designing his own automated sequences. He leveraged AI to write compelling sales copy in different tones: funny, authoritative, familiar, and friendly. He would test out various approaches, and when something worked, he would double down.

John single-handedly became the number one source of this company's new business. His bosses started giving him more money, higher commissions, then residual commissions. Without a marketing department, this company was now disproportionally reliant on John. He received a promotion and then a 2 percent equity stake in the company.

Five years later, John was making mid-six figures, and when the company sold for over $100 million, he received $2 million in cash and chose to stay on to continue to build the company for the new owner.

One day the original owners called John and asked for a meeting. They had decided to start another company and wanted John to be a cofounder, with a much larger equity stake.

John was now confident that he could generate sales for any company—all because he learned how to prospect. He learned how to generate sales without a marketing department, which made him incredibly valuable. Because of his skill set, he was able to write his own ticket, and his employers were more reliant on him than he was on them.

This is the power of becoming a competent prospector. It is the single most important skill set, yet it's the one sales skill that everyone tries to avoid by relying on a marketing department for leads.

If you get leads from a marketing department, great! But never be reliant on those leads alone. It's like a drug dealer giving away free samples in the hope that you will get addicted and come back and buy more. The more reliant you become on the marketing team, the angrier you'll get when the leads they provide aren't qualified or are low-quality or not a fit for your product or service.

You should treat any leads you receive as bonus leads. The top 20 percent of commission earners always prospect their own leads. Everyone else just accepts what they're given. Furthermore, marketing campaigns often change. The new messaging, new channels, and new marketing avatars change the quality of the leads, making them variable in quality. By relying on leads from the marketing department alone, you are allowing them to determine your income. Learn to prospect, and it will set you free.

Now let's get into it.

Prospecting is the most difficult part of the selling process. Most sales professionals spend 80 percent or more of their time prospecting for new customers. Prospecting is so difficult that a new business science was invented to contend with it: they call it *marketing*. What marketing attempts to do with content and money, a sales professional must do with time. Luckily, automation and AI now allow sales professionals to scale their time like never before.

The first step to successful prospecting is knowing whom to target. Identifying your target prospect is a multistage process that starts with asking yourself, "Who is my customer?" Your ability to answer that question with absolute clarity will determine your success or failure in attracting and closing new customers.

If you are currently in business, you can look at your past and current customers, find the common denominators, and use them as your first *prospect profile*.

The prospect profile is also commonly known as the *customer persona* or *avatar*. In marketing, a well-defined customer profile is essential for targeting marketing messages to the right people. Some sales professionals are only able to sell to people like themselves, so sometimes it makes sense to create a profile that mirrors yourself and then try to find people like you.

As the skill and art of selling have evolved, the line separating sales and marketing has blurred. Many sales professionals and business owners find themselves doing micromarketing campaigns to small groups of people. A micromarketing campaign involves making several strategic outreach attempts that are designed to achieve a specific result: for example, a prospect agrees to a free trial, redeems a coupon, confirms a meeting, or schedules an appointment.

Before you do any prospecting, you need to be very clear about your product or service offering. If you have trouble answering any of the questions below, you need to go to work at once so that you can say the answers even in your sleep. Here are the most important questions you must answer before attempting to have any contact with a prospect:

What is it? The first question anyone will ask themselves about your product or service is, "What is it?" You must be able to clearly articulate exactly what it is. Write it down in less than three sentences, then shorten it to two, then one. Now that you have a one-sentence answer, tell someone what it is. How do they react? Confused? Excited?

You must define with brevity what your product or service is. It must be so simple a child can understand and communicate that understanding to another child.

Here are two examples that illustrate the difference between clear and simple language and unnecessary and confusing language. The subject product is LinkedIn.

1. It's a collection of professionals that network online to increase meaningful business relationships for the purposes of business growth or explore employment opportunities.
2. It's a social network for business.

Which description is easier to say and understand? Obviously, example two. When selling anything, it's better to be understood quickly than to confuse people with elaborate and unnecessary explanations. The faster your prospect understands, the sooner you can move on to the next step.

Whom is it for? The second question is, "Whom is it for?" This question will help guide you to the right people and save you countless hours. We often don't really know whom our product is for until we find the *wrong* people. Eventually, one wrong person may know exactly whom we should target, and if you ask them, they will likely tell you. Don't be afraid to ask for a better contact if the person with whom you are speaking is uninterested.

Who will benefit from using your product or service? Who wants and needs the results it delivers? By achieving clarity on whom it's for, you will recognize your prospects faster, spend less time with the wrong people, and become more efficient in general.

If you find yourself struggling to find the right people, use the 100-call method: instead of contacting your prospects with the intention to sell something, contact them and ask for guidance. You can say something like, "Hi. I was hoping you could help me find the right person?" Explain what you do in terms of results, then ask them who would be the best person to contact. If they tell you, ask for their contact information. Alternatively, you can ask, "How does your company go about buying products like mine?"

If you make 100 contact attempts of this kind, on average you will speak to ten people. Seven of them will not be helpful, but three will be extremely helpful. They will tell you everything you need to know to find and contact the right people. They will teach you the industry jargon to use, how to describe the value you deliver, and what your initial ask should be. This one exercise can save you months of exasperation.

How does it work? If I told you there is one strategy that you can use today that will double your sales in less than ninety days, what question would you ask? Probably what is it, and how does it work? You would probably ask me how and persist, because if that result (for example, doubling sales in ninety days) is important to you, you will be very curious. This is commonly called a *curiosity hook*. It's something you can say that will cause your prospect to become very curious.

If someone asks you how your product or service works, it's important to only answer the question if you have the prospect's undivided attention and enough time to answer properly. Pay special attention to the Three Sales Method and appointment statement in the chapters ahead.

Why buy it? So why should anyone buy your product? There are only a few simple reasons why people buy anything:

1. They want the results your product or service delivers. People don't buy new software programs and spend onerous hours implementing them because they're fast, pretty, and easy to use. They buy software because of what it delivers in terms of increased productivity, time or cost savings, and the ability to make better, data-driven decisions. The buying drivers are to get more work completed, save time, save money, and be smarter.

2. They want the improvement your product or service delivers. People don't buy mobile phones because of their pixel density, processor type, or storage capacity. They buy smartphones because they want to see more on the screen, they want their apps to open fast, and they don't want to worry about maxing out their internal storage. The buying drivers are to see more, do more, and not to worry.

3. They want the status your product or service conveys. People don't buy Lamborghinis because they are practical. They don't hold much cargo or many people. A Lambo barely has any ground clearance, so the places you can go are limited. I suspect that most people who own a Lamborghini don't even drive it fast. They buy Lamborghinis because they draw attention, making the driver feel special and inflating their sense of status. Here the buying drivers are attention, feeling special, and status.

If you tried to sell something based on aesthetics, features, accessories, specifications, and warranty information, you would not sell much, if anything at all. Great sales professionals see the motivation behind the interest and cater to the core motives of their prospects. Although every prospect is slightly different, they all want results, improvement, and status.

Once you are clear on the basics of your product or service and market, you can start approaching your target prospects with a structured outreach strategy. There are many ways to contact potential prospects. Here is a partial list:

1. Create a landing page and lead magnet.
2. Scrape together a list of potential targets from the Internet.
3. Go to events, networking groups, conferences, and industry-specific trainings or workshops.
4. Physically walk into a business and start a conversation with the owner.
5. Knock on someone's front door.
6. Create and send direct mail.

7. Design an email outreach and cadence strategy. (A cadence strategy is a sequence of varied outreach methods that sales reps can use to engage prospects better.)
8. Buy a list from a local business journal or a marketing firm.
9. Call someone on the phone.
10. Stand on the corner with a big sign and wave.

When you read the list above, you probably cringed at a few options. As a sales professional, you must decide on the best approach and outreach strategy for your business. Ask yourself these questions:

Where are my prospects? Are they all in one zip or postal code? If so, direct mail doesn't sound like a bad idea. Are they located all over the world? Then maybe an Internet strategy makes the most sense.

What do my prospects do, like, or search for? If you know they like golf, take up golfing. If you know they love doughnuts, spend more time at doughnut shops. If they search for specific things on the Internet, design a Google Adwords campaign, and make sure you have a compelling landing page with a strong curiosity hook and compelling lead magnet (more on this later).

Ask yourself these key questions about your prospects and existing customers:
1. What do they fear? What keeps them up at night?
2. What do they hope for? What does their ideal future look like?
3. What do they most need to hear to become curious about your product or service?
4. What is the worst-case scenario for their business?
5. What is the best-case scenario for their business?

The Core Activities

FIND

Business owners and sales professionals must find their own prospects. Marketing departments serve this function for business owners, who often pass leads to their sales teams. If you're in sales or getting into a sales position, its advantageous to be at a company that can pass you leads and prospects. Having a lead machine pre-built and functioning allows sales professionals to focus on qualification, trust, discovery, presentation, and closing. If there are no leads or prospects, the sales professional's default mode needs to be finding prospects.

Even if you have a marketing department or blog that produces leads, a good business practice includes finding leads through outreach. Consider your ability to find and cultivate leads for your business as a diversification strategy. There are countless examples of businesses growing with a purely inbound strategy, but then competition erodes their advantage, stifling their growth. Be the person that leverages the leads you receive, but don't depend on them for sales and business growth. By being self-reliant and finding and closing business independently, you will make yourself extremely valuable to your organization.

ORGANIZE

As you build your prospect list, you must ask yourself what information you need about your prospects, such as name, phone number, email, location, address, gender, education, industry, and company name. Data is not always easy to find. It's important to pick your data points selectively, as each new data point can represent an onerous amount of work that might not be essential to your sales process. In my experience, the essential data points are:

- Name
- Phone number or email (you can get one with the other)
- Company
- Title

You can fill in everything else as you go.

Your prospect list is one of the most valuable investments you can make in yourself as a sales professional or business owner. Think of it like a bank account and each new contact as a deposit. Over time and with active management, a well-organized and updated prospect list is an appreciating asset representing current and future business: this is why you should invest your time and money into a CRM system the you enjoy using. The most popular of these is Salesforce.com, a cloud-based software platform that can accommodate a variety of business types.

The best CRM for your business is the one that you will use daily. The only way a CRM can truly benefit your business is if you use it frequently, keep it updated, and be consistent. There are countless examples of businesses who rush to launch and update their CRM, but only log in once a month.

The key benefit of a CRM system is its ability to ensure that nothing slips through the cracks. Everyone is contacted, appointments are set, presentations are completed, and you never miss a follow-up opportunity. For it to work, a CRM needs to become a digital extension of your brain. Which means you need to sync up with it as often as possible.

If you're a business owner, utilizing a CRM will help you offload sales responsibilities to new hires. A business owner's ability to step back from day-to-day sales responsibilities is the first step in truly scaling a business. If you are a business owner and still maintain most of the sales responsibilities, you don't have a business; you have a job.

The Three Sales Method

Now that you have well-organized and updated database of leads and prospects, you must contact them and get a meeting. This might be as simple as a phone call but often requires an email strategy. Expand your outreach options to social network direct messages (DMs), which allow you to send text messages; WhatsApp; WeChat; Telegram; iMessages; or whatever platform offers the most appropriate channel.

Because everyone is super busy and hyper distracted, you will need to master the *Three Sales Method*. I learned this after making the transition from business-to-consumer (B2C) sales to enterprise (business-to-business, or B2B) sales. I had just taken a job at a software startup and was given a desk and a database of names and phones numbers. I was making over 100 phone calls a day. I would get so excited when I thought the person on the phone was a prospect that I would immediately launch into a detailed explanation of our product. I didn't take a breath or pause. As you can imagine, those monologues were usually cut short by the clicking sound of disconnection. I call this "throwing up on the customer."

It took me a couple more weeks, but I finally figured it out. It turned out that I needed a whole new map, which I have termed the Three Sales Method. For every one successful sale, you actually need to make three separate sales.

1. The first sale you make is yourself: your experience and credibility. If you are lucky enough to work for a well-known brand, this will be easier for you. Simply saying, "Hi, it's Michael from Goldman Sachs" or "I'm with McKinsey and Company" could establish your credibility. It's also your voice: how relaxed and competent you sound, how friendly and conversational your tone is, and your rate of speech. Try smiling while you speak, and take some deep breaths before you introduce yourself. If your meeting is in person, make eye contact and shake hands confidently.
2. The second sale (which I was missing) is for time. You must become expert at getting time commitments. When you master selling for time, you will quickly start getting more and better results. What could you do with twice as many appointments? You could double your sales! And then do it again.
3. The third sale is for your product or service. Once you have the time to sit down with your prospect, you can ask good questions, discover pains and problems, and provide compelling insights.

If you do not have an adequate time commitment, you will not be able to complete your sales process. So how do you get more time commitments? How do you get more meetings?

The Appointment Statement

Before you can ask them to pay in money, you must get them to pay attention! You can do this with an *appointment statement*:
1. Introduce you and your company.
2. State whom you serve.
3. State the primary result you deliver.

The goal of a well-delivered appointment statement is to illicit the question "How?" How do you do that? How does it work?

For example: "Hi, my name is Michael Tracy, and I'm the founder of Sales Journey. I work with sales professionals, business owners, and entrepreneurs and help them double their sales in ninety days."

Completed correctly, your prospect should say either out loud or to themselves, "That's me! How?"

In my case, when they hear "sales professionals, business owners, and entrepreneurs," they'll say to themselves, "That's me. Michael serves people like me." When they hear, "Double sales in ninety days," they'll think, "How does he do that?" Then they'll ask, "How?"

When you receive a "how" response, you know you have designed your appointment statement well. The key is *not* to answer the question. This will be very difficult, because you will want to explain it all in that moment.

Instead, pause and say, "I'd love to show you how. Do you have some time on Thursday at 11 a.m.?" and close them on the appointment. Your goal is to convert curiosity into time. If you're not getting enough appointments, you need to generate more curiosity.

I had to try five different appointment statements before I got one to work consistently. But once it did, my calendar filled up with appointments, and I was able to double and then triple my sales performance in eight weeks.

Forge your appointment statement in the fire of the marketplace by trying it out at every opportunity. Repeat until it starts to work consistently. Once it works, use it everywhere: on the phone, in person, in your email signature, on your social profiles.

Only when you have an appointment can you qualify your prospect to determine their buying potential. Buying potential is composed of five criteria:
- Need
- Money
- Desire
- Timing
- Authority

These are also the core qualifying criteria in the next chapter. To turn a lead into a prospect and then into a viable opportunity, two of the five criteria need to be met. Once identified, prospects should be given information, education, and valuable content to further qualify them before a discovery conversation can take place.

qOS for AI Prompt Design

Utilize AI to create outreach copy, scripts, emails and any other relevant collateral. You can use a variation of qOS for prompt design. Here is how you can create an excellent prompt:

1. **Why: the goal of the prompt.** Example prompt: help me create a sequence of twelve emails that will enable me to confirm more appointments with my prospects.

2. **Who: the audience.** Example prompt: the prospects are sales professionals, business owners, and entrepreneurs that want to increase their sales and revenue with proven sales training techniques.

3. **What: specify the format of the desired content.** Example prompt: the emails should be short, three to five sentences, focused on the results I deliver, and should end with a question. Ask them to pick between two different days and times, and let them know that I will confirm with a calendar invite and link.

4. **How: any specific instructions.** Example prompt: the emails should increase in urgency while keeping a conversational and jovial tone. Each email should include an attention-grabbing subject line that motivates the recipient to click through.

5. **When: any time, specifics, and deadlines.** Example prompt: the emails will go out once per week for twelve weeks starting in mid-September and ending mid-December (specify year). Please make references to any relevant United States–based holidays.

6. **Where: any relevant location information.** Example prompt: All the recipients will be based in North America. Please specify Pacific Time in the emails when requesting appointments with specific times.

Then put it all together:

> Help create a sequence of twelve emails that will enable me to confirm more appointments with my prospects. The prospects are sales professionals, business owners, and entrepreneurs that want to increase their sales and revenue with proven sales training techniques. The emails should be short—three to five sentences—focused on the results I deliver, and should end with a question. Ask them to pick between two different days and times, and let them know that I will confirm with a calendar

invite and link. The emails should increase in urgency while keeping a conversational and jovial tone. Each email should include an attention-grabbing subject line that motivates the recipient to click through. The emails will go out once per week for twelve weeks, starting in mid-September and ending in mid-December of this year. Please make references to any relevant United States–based holidays. All the recipients will be based in North America. Please specify Pacific time in the emails when requesting appointments with specific times.

You can also ask AI to help you design your prompt. Replace the word "help" in the above prompt to "help me design the most effective prompt that will . . ."

You can use this format to create a variety of content. Use the qOS format to create images and videos too. AI is a massive productivity booster. AI is changing the game. It's allowing business owners and sale professionals to multiply their efforts.

Each step in the process can be optimized with AI.

If you need help, just ask. You can state your goal, then ask, "What additional information do you need from me to create a prompt that will achieve my goal?"

Cultivate and Nurture

Your database should be composed exclusively of leads, prospects, current customers, and past customers. It's ten times easier to resell to a current or past customer than it is to get a new customer, yet most sales professionals default to finding new customers to grow their book of business. Deciding in advance how you will maintain good relationships with existing and past customers can make a huge difference in your ability to get more sales and grow your business.

The other key is timing. You want to be there at the right time so that when a prospect is ready to make a buying decision, they think of your product, service, and company first. You accomplish this by maintaining a series of light-touch communications with valuable insights, updates, and positive impressions.

The worst mistake you can make is to qualify a prospect and then let them forget about you. Think like a marketer when it comes to contacting your leads and prospects. Marketers try to make ten to twelve positive impressions through different channels (like social media, email, mobile) to build familiarity and brand affinity, so that when the target of the marketing messages can buy, they choose your product. Think of the cereal aisle at your grocery store. Each box of cereal is a potential choice, but we often choose cereal we are already familiar with.

For sales professionals, each outreach or follow-up attempt should leave a positive impression; it should not be simply a request to buy or an inquiry about their status. Statements like "Are you ready now?" "Just checking in on the agreement" and "Did you decide yet?" will not help you get a sale. Instead, send them something of interest, like a recent article, a relevant YouTube video, or white paper. The culmination of those positive impressions will often lead them to buy your product or service when the time is right.

Maintain Your Database

Your database is an asset. I know of companies that have been sold solely for their database of prospects and customers. Treat your database like a vault filled with gold. Make sure to organize it; add details regularly; schedule reminders, tasks, and appointments; and add notes on every interaction. Each time you add to your database is like making a deposit in a bank account.

Update your CRM so clearly that you could have someone else take over seamlessly with your daily activities.

Your database should be pruned and cleaned up from time to time. If you know a prospect has moved to another business that you can't serve, delete them or move them to the freezer. The freezer is a term for the contacts in your database that have no present value, but potentially could be "defrosted" in the future if an opportunity arises.

The core activities of prospecting should be scheduled. Nobody defaults to prospecting as a task. Prospecting is difficult, sales professionals try to avoid it, and the activity haunts them at night. To beat back the fear and discomfort of prospecting, you must schedule it on your calendar. Block off time in the morning and the afternoon for prospecting. Label the appointment "Future Income Opportunities" and treat it seriously.

Here's a good schedule for prospecting:

The night before. Identify your targets and build your list with contact details. The worst thing you can do is wake up ready to prospect with no one to contact. You end up wasting your entire morning hunting for people to contact instead of actually contacting anyone. Make sure you do this data entry when it doesn't interrupt your flow during prime work time.

First thing in the morning. Before you check your email, start your prospecting activities: make thirty calls, send emails requesting appointments (more on this later). Start work first thing.

Resolve to work in two ninety-minute sprints in the morning. Top performers start their first ninety-minute sprint at 7 a.m., so they can finish both sprints as early as 10 a.m.

The afternoon. By this time, you should be mentally drained and your cognitive abilities will probably have been exhausted. Now you can check your email, follow up, and confirm meetings. Use any extra time to build your prospecting list for the next day. Save the morning for your most difficult tasks.

How to Time Prospecting Calls

What is the best time to cold-call potential prospects? I get this question all the time. Is there a time or day that is better for making prospecting calls? The answer is no. There is not a better time or day to make calls. It doesn't matter what time or day it is. If your prospect is awake, it's a good time to call.

I've conducted an informal study on the best times and days to make calls. I've interviewed many sales people and asked colleagues and other sales trainers. This is some of the feedback I've received:

1. You shouldn't call on Monday mornings because they've just got to the office and they're really busy.
2. You shouldn't call before 10 a.m., because they haven't settled in yet.
3. You shouldn't call between the hours of 12 and 2 p.m. because this is lunchtime or just after lunch. They're digesting their food and will be tired.
4. You shouldn't call them after 4 p.m. because they are wrapping up their day and would not welcome a disturbance at closing time.

5. If you are calling management, you shouldn't call on Monday afternoon, because they'll be preparing their teams for the week.
6. If you're calling technical staff, you shouldn't call them any morning, because that's when they get their best work completed.
7. If you're calling any government department, you shouldn't call on Mondays or Fridays.

It goes on, but you can see what's happening here. At some point, you start building in these rules, and they force you to exclude all but twelve hours a week when your prospects will be receptive to phone calls. That's just hogwash. If you have calls to make, make them and be done with it.

Also note that today, approximately 60 percent of all phone calls are automated. That means that most people will not pick up the phone the first time you call. Ten years ago, the prevailing wisdom was to never leave a voicemail message, as it would slow you down and be a waste of time. Today, leaving a voicemail is the only way to prove you're not a robot. When you leave a voicemail message, speak clearly and use your appointment statement. It's your job to generate curiosity, which will translate into a callback. Most voicemails are now transcribed and not necessarily listened to, so try to sound like a human being. If you read a script, make a mistake on purpose and correct yourself.

9

Qualifying Sales Prospects

If you want to grow your businesses and make more sales, you must interact with people who have a need and desire and can pay for our product or service. In addition, they must possess the authority to make a buying decision, and the timing must be correct.

These are the five main qualifying criteria for any prospect in any industry:

- Need
- Desire
- Money
- Authority
- Timing

Experienced business owners and sales professionals develop a keen sense that someone is qualified by developing targeted questions that cut through the fat and fluff that encompass the usual social graces.

Here are some excellent qualifying questions:
- When do you need to make this decision?
- Does anyone else need to be included in our meeting?
- What is your budget for products and services like these?
- How do you buy services like this?
- What is your buying process? Or, how do you buy products like this?
- How fast do you need a solution?
- Is price the most important consideration? If not, what else is?
- How long have you been in business?
- How many people does your company employ?

We could go on and on. Any one of these questions might fulfill multiple qualifying criteria. The key to using these five criteria is to understand that only two of five need to be met in the first interaction. That is, if you are speaking with someone who has a need and money but does not have desire, authority, or timing, they are still worth developing as a prospect. Your actions can make a difference for each of the core qualifying criteria.

Any given prospect will most likely lack one or more of the five criteria. A *need* is the only criterion that requires absolute clarity. You should only sell things that people really need. If you recognize that they don't need your product or service, you should politely wrap up and walk away. Often you will be presented with opportunities to sell to someone who does not need what you have. Refrain from selling to these people, because they will haunt your reputation for the rest of your life. Eventually, they will discover that they did not need your product or service, and they will never forget that you sold it to them anyway. It's always better to play the long game when your reputation is at stake.

You create a need with education. You can show the prospect that given their situation, they very much have a need for your product or service. Understanding your prospect will help you cultivate their need. The best sales professionals can make their products and services look indispensable by the time they have finished their presentation. We'll address this in more detail in the chapters ahead.

If the prospect does not have a *desire* or motivation to buy your product within a reasonable period, you can make it more desirable. How? To generate desire, try these techniques:

Juxtaposition. In the art world, to juxtapose something is to put it besides something else of the same nature to enhance its characteristics. Show your prospect your product next to your competitors'. Let them compare the two and appreciate the differences in appearance, quality, and ease of use. Allow them to explore the two products without your speaking or interrupting. Let them conclude for themselves that they prefer your product to the others.

Elevate your product's status. Show your prospect that other people with high status and authority use your product or service. Get pictures with celebrities using your product. Do whatever you can to associate it with high-status people and companies. Achieving a high-status reputation will allow you to charge a premium and maximize your profits and commissions.

Apple is a recent example. Their iPhones are consistently 30 percent more expensive than a comparable Android device. They can charge 30 percent more on status alone. People want to be associated with Apple products and the people that use them. In addition, Apple's iMessage displays blue message bubbles when two Apple iPhone users message each other. When an Android user is added to the conversation, the chat bubbles turn green. Apple has lowered the status of the Android user based on their green chat bubbles.

Manufacturers of luxury cars like Audi, Lexus, and Infiniti understand how to use status very well. These cars often share the same chassis, engines, and electronic systems as their less expensive, lower-status offerings, like VW (which owns Audi), Toyota (which owns Lexus), and Nissan (which owns Infiniti). By adding 10 percent more in features, aesthetics, and branding, they can charge 50 percent more for a vehicle with the same utility as their lower-status offerings. Louis Vuitton can charge over $2,000 for a leather handbag because of the status it conveys.

Tell a great story. Engage your prospect's emotive centers by telling a story that illustrates the deeper meaning behind your company and your product. Focus on your prospect, use a happy customer they can relate to, then paint a picture of how that customer purchased your product and received an amazing experience. Your goal should be to show your prospect that when they buy your product, they will also receive the resources, people, and good nature of your entire company. We will discuss how to create great stories later in this book.

One company that has leveraged this technique well is TOMS shoes. TOMS donates a pair of shoes to someone in need for every pair of shoes it sells. This is not only a wonderful story but a wonderful way to overcome price resistance. In addition, customers want to buy directly from TOMS instead of a third-party to make sure their shoes generate a donation.

Financial Alternatives

If your prospect does not have money, it's not the end. This can be surmounted in a variety of ways: financing, paying over time, providing a discount for referrals or a referral bonus. There are many creative ways to solve a lack of money. If they meet at least two other qualifying criteria, it's worth exploring the options.

In fact, there has never been a better time in human history for creative money solutions. There are so many options to leverage the future for the present that if you can show your product or service is associated with cost savings, productivity increases, or revenue growth, you can close the sale. Because money is the most common objection (price is too high, it's not in the budget, and so on), we will cover this extensively in the chapters ahead.

Authority

Authority is simply the power of the prospect to make a buying decision. Often you will be speaking to either an authority or an influencer. It's important to distinguish between the two early on.

If the prospect is the authority, they should be very comfortable stating that without ambiguity. Do not ask them, "Are you the authority?" because if they're not, they may lie to maintain their sense of status or ego. Instead ask, "Is there anyone else who should be included in our meeting?" or "Is there any other person that will want to weigh in on this decision?" These questions are less confrontational. There's an old quote: "If a person doesn't weigh in, they won't buy in." Make sure every stakeholder is present at a meeting where you expect to close.

If you are speaking with an influencer, ask them, "How do you like to buy products or services like this?" or "What's your buying process?" These questions acknowledge that there is a buying process. Even if there is not, the influencer will likely provide you with insights on how best to make the sale. With influencers, it's best to educate and empower them so that they can champion your product to others in their organization (or to their spouses).

Timing

Arguably the most important factor is, when? If you cannot make a sale to a prospect in a reasonable period, it may not be worth the effort. Markets, industries, and businesses change faster today than ever. Any sort of buying momentum you create today will not exist next week, next month, or next quarter. You must be highly aware of the prospect's buying time line. Ask them directly: "When do you plan on making a decision?" "When do you plan to buy this?"

Timing and follow-up go together like peanut butter and jelly. What does *following up* really mean? It's the collection of activities you do to be there *at the right time*. It's that simple. The most successful sales professionals have figured out how to follow up methodically without annoying their prospects. If you don't have a plan or system for following up with your prospects, you will not be there when the time is right, and you will lose sales to those who do have a plan and system in place. We will discuss follow-up systems later in this book.

The Qualifier Sales Method

This powerful method enables the sales professional to flip the power dynamic. If the prospect is demonstrating enough curiosity about your product or service, you should try this method. When someone demonstrates interest in your product or service, you may want to answer all the questions, show them all the results and benefits, address competitive issues, and get in front of objections. Some of us might even talk about pricing before we're asked. Yikes!

The qualifier sales method relies on specific questions framed correctly. The one thing you will need is the curiosity of your prospect. If they do not demonstrate curiosity, do not attempt this method. The prospect demonstrates curiosity by asking you questions about your product or service, such as certain features, benefits, or pricing.

Here's a sample dialogue of a sales professional using this method:

Prospect: Can you tell me about this feature? Benefit? Price?
Sales Pro: Yes, I can answer those questions, but first, do you mind if I ask you some questions?
Prospect: Yes, go ahead.
Sales Pro: Our company only works with very specific types of businesses. We've found that we can deliver great value, cost savings, productivity gains, and increased revenue, but only for the companies that match our specific criteria. May I ask you how many employees you have?
Prospect: Twenty-two.

Sales Pro: We typically like to work with companies with twenty-five or more employees. Tell me, is your company growing?

Prospect: Yes. We grew our revenue 35 percent last year and we're projecting to do the same or better this year.

Sales Pro: Great. Our service really only helps growing companies, so I'm glad to hear that. Time is another important criterion for us. We like to engage with companies who can make a buying decision within forty-five days. Do you have an immediate need for a service like ours?

Prospect: Yes, if we are clear that your service is right for us, we could buy it tomorrow.

Sales Pro: Excellent. Can you tell me about your company's capacity to integrate our services? We've found that we're most successful when our clients can appoint someone on their team to be 100 percent responsible for implementation. Do you have someone who can work with us until everything is up and running?

Prospect: Yes, absolutely. Shelly would be your point person and would be responsible.

Sales Pro: OK, thank you. Now let me show you how our service can work for your company.

In this hypothetical example of the qualifier sales method, the sales professional accomplished much more than you may realize:
1. The sales pro reversed the power dynamic by creating a desire in the prospect to qualify for the service.
2. The sales pro was able to ask all the most important qualification questions in the context of exclusion as opposed to inclusion. That is, the sales pro was actively trying to *disqualify*

the prospect, thereby forcing them to really want to meet the criteria. The alternative is to have the prospect qualify you or your company, forcing you to defend, talk too much, and show too much too soon.

3. The sales pro elevated their company by making it seem more exclusive and selective than its competitors, and as a result increased the perceived value of its products and services.
4. The sales pro highlighted a nonqualifying metric (the number of employees) but made an exception based on the company's growth rate. This brings the sales pro and the prospect closer together in the spirit of collaboration.
5. The sales pro protected their time and the time of their prospect by qualifying rigorously up front. This suggests to the prospect that the sales pro's time is very valuable, and that the pro has many other opportunities to pursue.
6. Once the prospect felt that they were qualified, they felt accepted and validated, which creates positive rapport.
7. The sales pro was able to help the prospect imagine what would happen after the sale by highlighting implementation and seeding an ongoing relationship with Shelly, the point person, who can now be contacted directly.

This powerful tactic can be used when enough curiosity has been demonstrated by the prospect, but it can *only* be used in the beginning of the relationship and before the discovery process.

At the end of this method, as an alternative to launching into a discovery session or presentation, try closing the appointment, which can secure the time you will need to complete the sale. You can say something like, "This is really great; you look like the ideal client for our company. The next step is for us to schedule a meeting so that we can understand your business better. Then we can present you with the right combination of services that make the most sense for you. Does next Thursday at 1 p.m. work for you?"

Be flexible in your qualification criteria. You alone know your minimum requirements, so it's important to customize the criteria based on what you know about each prospect. During this process you must show the prospect that they just barely qualify but that exceptions can be made for any deficiencies. In the hypothetical above, the number of employees required was not met by the prospect, but the growth rate was met. This is something you can point out during the conversation: "You don't meet our employee requirements, but your growth rate is excellent, so I'm sure I can make an exception in this case."

Automate Your Qualification Process

I've worked with many types of businesses over the years. The biggest problem for most of them is a lack of qualified prospects. Some businesses receive hundreds of leads every day, but most are unqualified. We see this frequently with businesses with excellent content marketing, great blogs, and quality information. The problem then is, how do you sift through and find only the most qualified prospects with whom to spend your valuable time?

The solution is to automate your qualification process. This can be accomplished in the same place you are capturing your leads. For simplicity, let's refer to lead capture on the Internet.

If you are generating traffic to your contact form through paid search or great content, you have some very effective options available to you. In Internet marketing, marketers use funnels to visualize the flow of leads.

As already noted, it's proven that the more information you require on your contact form or lead magnet capture form, the fewer submissions you will receive. Nevertheless, the simplest way to reduce the number of unqualified prospects is to increase the required amount of information requested. When you do this, you may also lose some qualified prospects who don't want to provide the additional information, so you will get less leads but more qualified leads. The key question is: if you don't have time to follow up with all of them anyway, are you losing any opportunities or more efficiently using your time?

Buyer Types

Understanding the different types of buyers will help you structure every part of your sales strategy. In my experience, I have encountered five distinct types of buyers: *impulsive, consensus, analytical, emotional,* and *decisive.*

IMPULSIVE BUYERS

Impulsive buyers will be overly enthusiastic about making a quick decision. They won't ask many questions, or they won't ask the right questions. They'll seem too eager. This type of buyer will only get you into trouble. With them, you will want to ask extra clarification questions. Make sure they have a real need for your product or service before you sell it to them. Ask if anyone else needs to be included in the purchasing decision. Thoroughly use due diligence on them before moving forward.

Here's why: These types of buyers will be the first to ask for a refund. They'll be the first to return the product, and they will usually not be happy once the euphoria of the purchase is over.

Your goal is to make sales only to customers who can become great referral sources for your business. With impulsive buyers, you must be extremely confident that they will receive more value than the actual cost. Make sure they or someone they employ is willing to implement, connect, install, or utilize your product appropriately.

CONSENSUS BUYERS

These buyers are the huge time wasters. They will pretend they have absolute and final authority to make a buying decision. You will spend lots of time speaking, presenting, and asking and answering questions. Then you get to the closing decision only to find that there is another person that needs to be in on it. You'll come back, repeat the process again, and it will happen again: another person should also be included. You'll go through the process again and again, and never receive a commitment or buying decision.

I call these consensus buyers because they view the decision to buy as a commitment that they are unwilling to make because it represents a risk. These buyers will try to disperse the risk to as many people as possible to insulate themselves in case the purchase doesn't work out. Make sure you ask up front if any other people should be included. You should ask in a way that enables the buyer to still pretend that they have absolute authority. Ask, "Is there anyone else that would enjoy seeing this presentation?" or "Is there someone that will using this product other than you that may be curious how it works?" Also set a time anchor. Ask, "What is your timeline for making a decision?" Finally, be prepared to walk (sometimes run) away and spend your time more effectively somewhere else.

ANALYTICAL BUYERS

Analytical buyers will want to see the data—the proof. Be prepared for them with testimonials from other analytical buyers, quoting actual numbers, percentage changes, or other hard facts.

Analytical buyers will want to see graphs, spreadsheets, industry-specific studies, and other sources whose data can power their comparative analysis machine. They will probably already have a spreadsheet with key data points. Help them fill in the missing information. If you work in technology, science, or engineering, befriend an engineer or other quant that can communicate directly with your prospect. Appealing to emotions, frustrations, and opinions can backfire. Ask questions like, "Are there any other data points you would like to see?" and "What kind of information would you like me to send you to help you make the best decision?"

Let the data sell, and if it doesn't, ask what it was about the data that made the prospect decide not to buy. This will provide you and your company with valuable business intelligence.

EMOTIONAL BUYERS

Emotional buyers love stories. Tell the story of why the company was created. Transform the executive staff into heroes on an important mission, fighting against the status quo. (Make sure you don't disparage your competitors). Make the world (which is not changing fast enough) the villain and your company the brave crew tackling the challenge. Use testimonial stories; use the first names of customers that you helped; highlight their initial state as overwhelmed, underperforming, in pain, or out of sorts. Then you grabbed their hand and led them through the bleak forest into a lush garden where all their problems were solved. Highlight their current state in terms of your current close relationship and all the referrals you now receive from your new fan.

Highlight how you would like to have a similar relationship with the prospect one day. In your presentation, use visualization exercises so that they can see a brighter future seamlessly using your service to get the benefits that you have described. Paint them a picture with your words.

DECISIVE BUYERS

God loves a decisive buyer. These are by far the best types of buyer. They're usually very busy, so it might take some time to get a meeting, but when you do, it will be straight, to the point, and short. The decision will come quickly and decisively, likely far faster that you anticipate. Usually in the middle of your presentation, they will stop you and say, "OK, let's do it" or "All right, we'll try it."

The usual reaction is to not fully believe they are ready to buy. In the past, I would just continue the presentation, and they would stare at me impatiently until I realized that they just wanted me to start the paperwork. Charge their credit card, send them the agreement, or whatever the next step would be. In this case, just go right into closing the sale. There may be a few questions during this process. Answer them, and continue your closing process. Do not talk your way past the sale by continuing your presentation. Just close the deal and fulfill the promise.

Key Questions

Do you have the capability of successfully selling to each of the above buyer types? Have you created the materials or crafted the stories necessary to influence a buying decision from an analytical, emotional, or decisive buyer?

If you answered no to any of the above questions, put this book down and act now! Preparation is 50 percent of the sale.

10

Building Trust

TRUST IS THE MOST precious commodity in business and in life. Your ability to earn the trust of your prospect is essential to your long-term success. Trust can be both easily attained and quickly lost. If it is lost, the relationship will never be the same. At this point, even if you somehow convince your prospect you are trustworthy again, you will not have the same level of trust you initially received.

There is an old saying: "A person convinced against their will is of the same opinion still." It means that many will pretend to believe you until you leave but still will not trust you. If trust is lost, consider doing whatever is necessary to win the confidence of your prospect back to your side. Any one prospect can influence hundreds of people, especially if they are well-known in their industry.

This ties back to both the value and the fragility of your reputation. Your reputation is trust (or lack thereof). A reputation for being trustworthy will precede you everywhere you go. It will open doors, secure high-value relationships, and ensure that you are paid more than your counterparts. It will also enable you to charge a premium.

When people speak of branding, they are referring to the trust placed upon the name and symbols of a company. The Nike logo, the swoosh, enables Nike to charge 500 percent more than their shoes cost to manufacture. Other companies with the same or higher-quality shoes wish their brand enjoyed as much trust as Nike. The key to bigger profit margins isn't always more or better products. Sometimes it's investing heavily in elevating the value of the brand.

Think of yourself as your own personal brand manager. Every decision you make increases or decreases the value of your brand to the world. The most brand-conscious business owners and professionals will always sacrifice short-term gains if the long-term consequences could potentially damage their brand.

If you are or have worked at a company with a well-known brand, you know how valuable it is when conducting business. The mere mention of a recognized brand name can establish enough trust for business and sales to transpire. If your company is not well-known, you will need to do much more.

The Trust Triangle

Luckily, there is a simple recipe for building high trust very quickly. I discovered this recipe in the early days of my career, and now I can immediately identify real professionals, because they all use a version this technique. I call it the *trust triangle*. A triangle, known as the shape of strength, is the ideal symbol to represent trust. The three points on the trust triangle represent the three keys to disarming criticisms in your prospect; they are *experience, testimonials,* and *references*. These can be translated into *confidence, social proof,* and *validation* respectively.

Building Trust

Every prospect will need all three of these to completely trust you. The three aspects of trust can be presented in a variety of ways. The type of presentation is less important than the timing of delivery, but the faster you can demonstrate these three keys to your prospect, the better.

Recently, I was evaluating different companies to install solar panels on my house. I would have them come to my home, measure the space and angle of my roof, and provide me with a quote for the solar system, installation, and city approval. One company asked if they could present their proposal in person, so I agreed, and we scheduled a meeting. The sales professional showed up dressed in the company's branded clothes. They suggested that we sit down so that they could show me their recommendation. Before they handed me the proposal, they handed me a packet of papers. The sales professional said, "Before we get started, I would like you to have this information." I immediately started flipping through this packet. The first few pages elaborated on the company's history and its founding. It was followed by pictures and explanations of their larger projects, generating *confidence*.

The next five pages were testimonials from residential customers like me. The testimonials were printed on the front and back. There were at least twenty, far too many for me to read in that sitting: *social proof*.

At the end of the packet were a list of ten references with email addresses and phone numbers: *validation*.

I looked through that packet for less than a minute, set it to the side, and asked to see the proposal. It wasn't the least expensive option, but I decided to go with that company because I had confidence that they could do a great job and complete it on time.

This is the power of the trust triangle. It can take the form of a packet of papers, a website, a brochure, or a video, or it can be delivered in any way that is appropriate for your business. Again, it must accomplish these three prerequisites:

Confidence. This is a demonstration of your experience. You must show that you are competent and accomplished in the product or service you are selling. You can show pictures of projects, videos of implementations, and links to previous and existing customers that show your work and substantiate your credibility.

Social proof. These are testimonials collected from happy customers. They can be written or audio or video recordings. The key point is to ensure that when your prospects read the testimonials, they can immediately relate to them. In their mind they should be saying, "These people are just like me." The testimonials should address different concerns that are common to your prospects. This approach can forestall many objections that may surface during the presentation and closing stages.

Validation. These are your references: third-party verification that what you say is true and that you can do what you say. References are an enormous source of comfort for a prospective customer. You must provide references in advance of being asked, or immediately upon request. A long interval between a request for references and their delivery correlates to a substantial decrease in trust and credibility.

Think of it this way: You are about to make a buying decision, but as a competent adult, you know you should check references before making a commitment to purchase. You ask, "Can you provide me with some references?" The sales professional says, "Yes,

I will send them over right away." Now think about your level of trust after just one hour of waiting. How about after two hours? Three? What if you don't get the references until the next day? For every minute you wait for them, you are losing trust and confidence in the company, the product, and the sales professional. Eventually you will lose trust and be unable to make a buying decision.

Therefore, it's paramount to prepare references in advance of any sales presentation or meeting with a prospective customer. Email or call existing customers and say, "Are you happy with your product, service, or experience?" If they say, "Yes, I am happy," ask them if they would be willing to be a reference and/or provide a testimonial. If they say, "No, I am not happy," then solve their problem, address their issue, and make them happy. The key question when you call an existing customer is "Are you happy?" The answer will determine your next action. Do not forget to ask this question.

From Fear to Hope

In this process, you are essentially moving your prospect from fear to hope. Here is one way to visualize it:

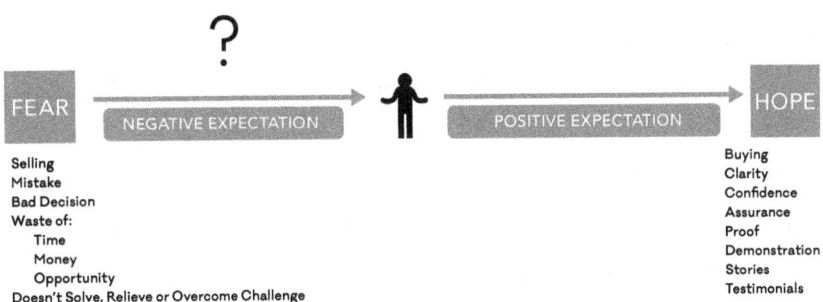

Fear and hope are the two primary emotions involved in buying behavior. Fear holds people back from taking risks, because it entails a negative expectation of the future. Hope provides the motivation to buy, because hope embodies a positive expectation of the future. These two emotions explain all the ups and downs on the stock market. The price of a company's shares represents its future, not its current state. If expectations for the future are positive, the price reflects hope. When a solid company's stock is severely punished even though it is fundamentally doing well, the market is responding to expectations for the future—in this case, fear.

Your job is to move your prospect from a state of fear to a state of hope. You must assume every prospect begins in a state of fear: they will be skeptical of you, your product or service, and your prices. Before you can guide your prospect to a hopeful future, you must understand what that future looks like to them. It would be a mistake to assume you already know, because everyone is different.

You begin by moving your prospect from fear to a neutral center position by using well-designed questions. (We'll go into detail about questions in chapter 12, which is about discovery.) Once they are in the neutral position, you need to move them all the way to the right until they view your product or service as necessary for a hopeful future.

There are two rightward thrusts in the diagram, and they each require a different set of skills. You must master both. The first rightward movement involves asking well-designed questions. Questions can demonstrate your competence, insight, and depth of knowledge. Once your prospect trusts you as a representative of your product, you can start the second rightward thrust. This involves empowering your prospect with insights, solutions, and relief, exposing them to the hopeful future that exists on the other side of a buying decision.

The Skill of Listening

Before we move on, we need to cover the skill of listening. This is by far the best, fastest, and most effective way to learn about your prospect and build trust at the same time. Twenty minutes of uninterrupted listening will build more trust than any amount of talking.

Listening is both a sense and a skill. My wife taught me this lesson and continues to remind me of it whenever she asks, "Michael, I know you're hearing me, but are you listening?"

The issue is that the human brain can process about 500 words per minute, but the average person only speaks at 150 words per minute. Even if we are listening intently, it still leaves us with 70 percent of the brain's capacity to think about other things.

To fully leverage our brain while listening, use a pen and paper. Listen to everything the speaker says with the intent of discovering some new piece of information—some problem, challenge, or pain. Actively write down the words as they are being spoken in real time. Only then can you utilize 100 percent of your brain. This will ensure that you don't miss a key point, insight, problem, challenge, or pain, missing any one of which could cause your presentation to miss the mark and thwart your ability to close the sale.

Business to Business Selling (B2B)

A note on selling business to business (B2B), especially to medium-sized and large businesses. Most large enterprises realize that human beings are fallible and that their ability to make objective decisions can be compromised. To add objectivity to a purchasing decision, many stakeholders in the company contribute to the creation of an elaborate RFI/RFP (request for information/request for proposal) process. This process is supposed to ensure that no bias enters the buying decision. The RFI/RFP procedure attempts to remove the psychology from the buying process and instead focus on company health (length of time in business, cash flow, current and happy customers), capabilities, composition of the team, scalability, and service levels.

If you are selling into enterprise companies, rest assured that you can still take tactical actions that will create a positive bias for your company. Here are a few of them:

1. Take every opportunity to contact the company. There are usually question-and-answer time periods before proposals need to be submitted. Use these to submit thoughtful and compelling questions. Your questions can demonstrate your knowledge and expertise, sometimes more than your answers on the RFP. If and whenever possible, schedule a meeting with someone on the buying team. Get to know them and humanize yourself. Find something you both can relate to, like golf, kids, dogs, food, or travel. Associating your company with a human being will bias them in your favor.

2. Realize that the prospect will go through your proposal with a checklist. You need to help them to check every box on that list. Answer all the questions, repeat the questions in your answer, and answer the question that is being asked. Make no assumptions. This is a procedural process, not a beauty contest. The checklist is the objective portion of the process; make sure your answers are not subjective in any way.

3. You cannot send gifts, but you can express gratitude in a variety of ways. Send the prospect emails with appreciative statements as often as possible. In any phone calls, tell them how grateful you are for their time and this opportunity. As soon as you are selected to submit an RFP, send them a physical card thanking them for selecting your company. Send them another after you make the submission, and another after they make the selection, even if they did not select your company. This will make you stand out and increase their positive feelings about your company, which will pay dividends in the future. Frequently, selected companies may not be able to fulfill their proposal, or not in a timely manner. They can also try to renegotiate their fees or fall out with the prospect in some other way. Expressing gratitude throughout the process, even in the face of rejection, will help bias them in your favor.

The Friendship Formula

Jack Schafer, a retired FBI agent, popularized the friendship formula in his book *The Like Switch: An Ex-FBI Agent's Guide to Influencing, Attracting, and Winning People Over*. He used it to recruit spies for the US government. The formula offers a clear way to create high-trust relationships. Like a math equation, the formula has four variables:

Proximity + Frequency + Duration + Intensity = Relationship

Proximity. This is how close you are physically to the person you want a relationship with. Have they seen you? Would they recognize you if they saw you again?

Frequency. This is how often you are around this person. It could include your local coffee shop, yoga class, or your office.

Duration. How much time do you spend with them? Five minutes or an hour? One on one? Or in a group?

Intensity. What is the nature of the experience you are sharing? Is it actively involved or passive?

You can take any person with whom you want a better relationship and grade yourself on each of these four factors. Go to work on your lowest grade until you have a better relationship.

If you can, try to plan an intense experience, like a whole day of golfing, skiing, or travel. These intense activities can create great relationships that last for years.

One of the best things you can do when you first sit down with a potential prospect is to not mention business until your prospect brings it up. Just sit down and act as if you're having a conversation with an old friend. If you've previously stated your intention to do business when you confirmed the appointment, then you don't need to launch into a business discussion immediately. Try to get to know them. Use this opportunity to speak about your interests, family, and future. All business is based on relationships, and relationships are personal.

The Five-Star Phenomenon

Millions upon millions of dollars have been spent commodifying trust. Large companies like Amazon, Uber, Yelp, and countless others have all adopted this strategy. They have distilled trust into a simple construct that includes five simple stars. Five stars in today's marketplace is the ultimate symbol of trust. All the hard work has been done for you.

You don't have to explain your rating system, but you do need to embrace it. Use five stars on your marketing materials, website, and product listings. Seek out reviews from your current customers, and ask them if they would give you five stars. Simply placing five stars next to your company name has an incredible subconscious impact. Take advantage of the five-star phenomenon.

The Advanced Appointment Statement

Have you ever played a video game and found a shortcut, like a tunnel or a door that launches you to the end of the level? In sales, the *advanced appointment statement* is the closest you'll get to a shortcut. It can launch you to the last 10 percent of the sale.

Nothing is more powerful than a true story of success. Take every customer success and turn it into a testimonial story. A testimonial story highlights a specific type of prospect, their problem, the solution, and the ongoing benefit. I have three prospect types: business owners, entrepreneurs, and sales professionals. For each type, I have several testimonial stories that I can use if a situation arises.

Here is the format for the advanced appointment statement. It's an expansion of the appointment statement we covered in chapter 8.

1. Introduce yourself and your company.
2. State the prospect type of the person you are speaking to.

3. Tell your testimonial story, including:
   - The specific problem your prospect was having
   - The discovery of the solution
   - The implementation of the solution
   - The ongoing benefits and results
4. Ask for a meeting so that you can show them how you did it.

Here's an example of a testimonial story. For context, I was at a conference and had just delivered a short presentation on sales training. I was speaking to a gentleman who was talking about his business (prospect type: business owner). I interjected this story in the conversation:

> You know, you remind me of my client John, who is a business owner just like you. John was the best salesperson at his company, as are many business owners I work with. He had hit a plateau growing his business. So we sat down together and discovered that he didn't have any salespeople, no onboarding process, no sales training plan, and no way to measure performance, not even his own. Within a couple weeks, we had created an onboarding process and sales training plan and started using a simple CRM for performance tracking.
>
> Within the month, he hired two salespeople. They went through the process we created and after couple months, one of the new hires was selling more than John. John stepped back from his selling responsibilities and was finally able to start thinking strategically about his business. He started to scale and expanded his market share. Last we spoke, he had rented a larger warehouse and hired two more salespeople.

> If you can relate to John, then I'd love to sit down and show you how we did it. Do you have availability next week? How about Tuesday at 11 a.m.?

Unlike the appointment statement, which results in a discovery meeting, the advanced appointment statement results in a verification meeting. If, after having heard your testimonial story, the prospect agrees to a meeting, it means they want the same result you illustrated in your story. The meeting will be to verify that your story is true. If you can prove your story is true, you are very likely to make a sale.

When you go to a verification meeting, bring all the materials you'll need to prove that what you said is true. When I went to this verification meeting, I brought my standard onboarding process and sample sales training plan, and I was prepared to demonstrate some CRM options. Most importantly, I brought a reference: John's contact information.

Use true stories that can be verified. If you don't have any of your own, borrow them from your company and use a company reference. It's easy to change the words in a testimonial story to say, "When our company start working with John" instead of "When I started working with John."

After some big wins of your own, you'll have all the testimonial stories you'll need to be a smashing success.

11

Insight Selling: Why It's the Future

As discussed earlier, sales methodologies have changed fundamentally in the last forty years. Your prospective customers are doing much of the work that was previously associated with the selling profession. As a sales professional, when you do finally engage with a qualified prospect, that prospect has likely discovered your company online, evaluated your products and services, read some reviews, read an article or two on your blog, and is now finally ready to ask questions and receive answers from a real human being.

In short, prospective customers have never been better informed than they are today. The level of information that is available to them is extraordinary. It is also very likely that they have created a short list of viable companies by the time they contact you and they are trying to eliminate the least desirable options. Your job is to show that your company has the best understanding of their problem, pain, or challenge. But how?

This is when a well-delivered insight can make all the difference. First, let's clarify: what is an insight? *An insight is something that elevates the understanding of your prospect.* A new understanding of their problem can help differentiate your product and differentiate yourself as an expert. When you have that first contact, it's important to realize that the prospect has likely been analyzing an enormous amount of information, analyzing different solutions, and comparing features, prices, and other factors. They desperately need someone to provide a clear perspective and illuminate the situation in a new way.

The selling profession has changed to accommodate new buying behavior. The chart below maps the current buyer's journey:

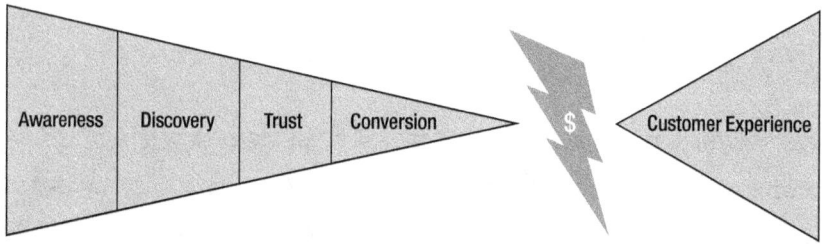

Awareness. This is when your advertising, email outreach, phone calls, social mentions, or marketing campaigns spark some interest. This also catalyzes the prospect to look for more information about your company's product or service.

Discovery. From the buyer's perspective, this is how easy it is to find additional information about your product or service, usually from your website or blog. Therefore, any marketing or outreach campaign needs to be consistent with the information on your website or social pages. The most common way to lose the prospect's interest is to spark their interest and drive them to a website or landing page that doesn't satisfy their curiosity.

Trust. This is the part where your prospect conducts an informal investigation. They will review your website, social pages, read reviews, and potentially compare you to your competitors. When you review your web and social pages, make sure they stack up better than those of your competitors.

Conversion. This is the part where you can really make a difference. Most prospects will not be willing to speak to anyone until this phase of the buyer's journey is reached. When you engage your prospect here, you will need to use your best insights. Insights will empower and motivate the prospect to buy, and buy from you specifically.

Customer experience. After a sale is made, the only way to get multiple sales and referrals is to provide an excellent customer experience. The customer must be so delighted with your company that they will buy again and tell their friends. This means fast and quality service, transparent and helpful account managers and customer service agents, and company policies that are easy to understand.

How to Develop Insights

Decide today to become an expert in your field. That means reading as much as possible about your industry, business, product, or service. You must understand the underlying trends in your industry and the larger economy. Attend events and absorb insights that are too fresh to be published. Clearly understand your competitors, their positioning strategy, strengths and weaknesses.

It's like getting a master's degree, only there is no end to your education. The rate of change is increasing more rapidly now than at any other time in human history. That means that what's true today will not be next year and may not be next week. This is a graph showing the technological innovation over approximately the last 750 years:

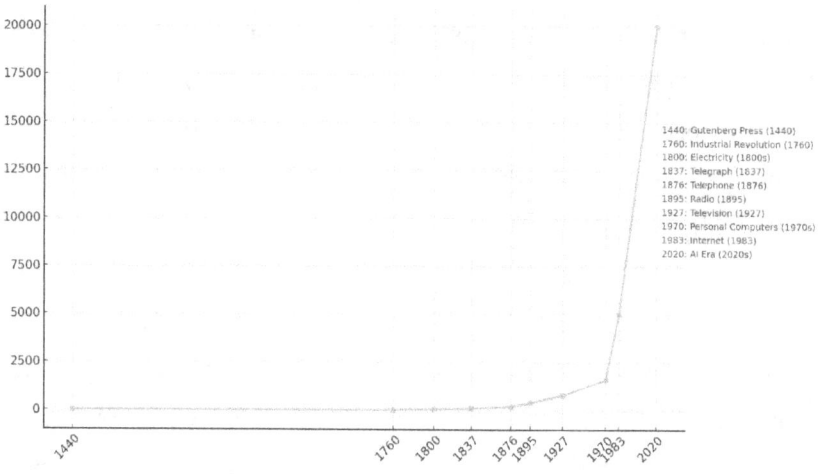

As you can see, we live in a time of rapid change. The supercomputer that we carry in our pocket has access to practically all human knowledge. We're instantly connected to billions of other people, financial markets that never sleep, and a twenty-four-hour information super cycle that never quits.

The most important skill for the future is to glean insights from this mess and successfully communicate these insights when and where it matters the most. In short, you will grow your business and income by gleaning insights that will help you sell your products and services.

The only way to elevate the understanding of others is to first elevate your own understanding. You must teach from a position of knowing, and that is only possible with study and work. There is a massive upside to all this study and work. Once you achieve an expert level understanding of your business, you will be seen differently. You will be able to get past gatekeepers, confirm more appointments, control the power dynamic in the presentation, and charge more for your products and services.

As an exercise, identify at least one event, publication, or timely book that is specifically related to your industry, product, or service. Then resolve to attend the event or read the material on a weekly basis. In-person events allow you to collect insights in real time instead of waiting for them to be published. When reading, underline or write down key points. When you have an aha! moment indicating a relevant insight, reverse-engineer the insight by identifying what you learned to attain it. Then develop a lesson that will allow you to teach it to your prospect.

When you teach valuable insights to your prospects, several wonderful things happen: you differentiate yourself as an expert, you provide practical value that creates reciprocity, and you empower your prospect with a higher level of understanding that enables them to stand out among their peers and colleagues.

Now that you are seen as an expert, the remainder of your presentation and follow-up interactions will be met with more consideration and respect. Any recommendations you make will be received more seriously. Moreover, if you close the sale, this prospect will have more confidence to recommend you and refer more business to you.

When you deliver something of value up front, you create reciprocity. Reciprocity is essentially an unwritten ledger, the balance of which is intuitively felt and monitored. If your prospect receives value from you, their indebtedness to you grows. If you continue to provide value without compensation, the tension to balance the ledger will eventually catalyze a buying decision. This is another way a valuable insight can help you close more sales.

When you teach your prospect something of value about their business, they will likely try to bring that level of understanding back to the stakeholders associated with the buying decision. This will make your prospect look like an expert, or at least like someone who has done their homework. When you elevate your prospect's status, they will see you with positive regard, which could last for years.

The Epiphany Process

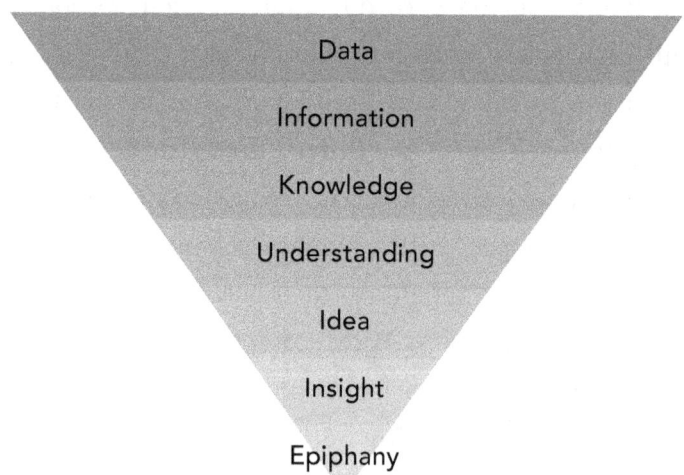

The above diagram depicts how data converts into insight. Data is the by-product of what the world and economy are doing every second. And it's being produced at staggering rates. At the time of this writing, data is being produced at some 2.5 quintillion bytes *per day*. That's 2,500,000,000,000,000,000 bytes per day!

When data is organized, it creates information. As you analyze information, like sorting a spreadsheet by specific variables, you can start to decipher patterns and trends. These patterns and trends tell you what has happened and allows you to estimate what might happen. This is knowledge.

When you connect one or more bodies of knowledge together, you achieve a deeper level of understanding. This deeper understanding starts to inform your own ideas about the world: your belief systems, opinions, and thoughts. A collection of related ideas is an ideology.

When an idea confirms, validates, or invalidates another idea that you possess, you have an insight. As you study and learn more, you form more ideas, a new idea competes with an old idea, and the best one wins. If a new idea wins, you have an insight which forces you to reevaluate other connected ideas. The ideas in your mind are like a market economy, where new companies compete with older, more established companies for resources and customers. In the mind, resources and customers can be equated with attention and conviction respectively.

When a new idea wins and you have an insight, that insight may force you to reevaluate a collection of interconnected ideas. In this case, your entire ideology may need to change to accommodate the new insight. Or an insight may initiate a sudden connection of several ideas all at once. This is commonly called an *epiphany* or *paradigm shift*. After an epiphany, you are no longer the same person: the way you view the world has fundamentally changed. It's like seeing the world in infrared instead of the normal visual spectrum.

An epiphany represents a sudden and giant leap in understanding. Understanding, like a rachet, only travels in one direction. For better or worse, no one can go back to their previous state of ignorance.

The bleeding edge of the epiphany process is moving from knowledge to understanding through experience (or action). This part of the process requires the most work. What is the most efficient way to develop new ideas? Long-form reading: *books*. The big ideas are found in big books. Unfortunately, in our fast-moving, superconnected, hyperdistracted world, the patience for long-form reading is waning. Books are conversations with very smart people, some living, some not; they are repositories of knowledge waiting to be understood. Supercomputers and even the most advanced AI cannot truly understand an idea. You can. By attempting to grasp the big ideas, you can position yourself to have the greatest number of epiphanies. Remember to read with a pen in your hand.

The late Mortimer J. Adler, the acclaimed author and liberal arts educator, would challenge his students to read difficult books. Even if the student could only understand 10 percent, it would still be worth the read. The next time the student read the book, their understanding would shoot to 50 percent, and the third time, to 90 percent comprehension. Tackling difficult books forces you to think, creates new connections in your brain, and expands your intellect in new and exciting ways.

To continually develop more and better insights, you must vigilantly study your craft, industry, business, and products. Using the epiphany process can help accelerate the development of insights. A well-delivered insight can make all the difference in increasing your sales and adding value to your organization.

How to Teach Insights

How do you transfer your level of understanding to a client or prospect? The first element is to determine the prospect's current level of understanding. You may be speaking with someone who is very well-informed and knowledgeable, in which case your insight transfer will be less of a challenge. If, as is more common, your prospect lacks enough understanding to be affected by your insight, you need to help elevate their understanding by teaching.

The first step is to ask a series of questions that enables you to estimate your prospect's level of understanding. The questions you ask will allow you to teach the right lesson.

In twentieth-century warfare, mortars were essential elements in artillery. Mortars are ground-mounted cannons that shoot up and arch to explode on an enemy position. In combat, it was frequent practice to fire three volleys. The first would go over the target and miss. The next shot, to correct the misguided first shot, would usually land in front of the target. This would enable the mortar team to choose the spot between the first two and greatly improve the accuracy of the third shot.

Your questions are like mortars: your first will assume too much understanding, the next too little, and then you will know the right questions to ask and lessons to teach.

Questions should not be interrogations: they should be worked naturally into a conversation. It's important to have your questions answered in a genuine way. Some people may pretend to understand more than they do in order to save face, maintain status, or keep authority.

Here are some of my sample questions in a sales context:
- Do you use the sales velocity equation to identify and improve your customer acquisition process?
- What is your customer acquisition cost?
- What is the lifetime value of your customer?
- What is the average lead time on your sales?
- What is your sales process?
- How do you generate leads?
- Whom do you consider a well-qualified prospect?
- What is your biggest constraint to increasing revenue?
- What is the composition of your sales team? SDRs? BDRs? SMs? SPs?
- How much of your business is derived from referrals?
- What is your cost of sales?
- What is your onboarding training plan?
- What are your KPIs?
- Do you use automation or AI for outreach or follow-up?

Many of these terms—particularly the acronyms—are commonly used in sales and business contexts: SDRs are sales development representatives, whose sole job is prospecting. BDRs are business development representatives, who are responsible for generating new business opportunities for the organization. SMs are sales managers. SPs are selling prices. KPIs are key performance indicators. The prospect's familiarity with such terms (or lack of it) will give you important insights into their level of understanding.

Your prospect will usually know some of the answers to your questions, but not all. Each time you identify a question that your prospect cannot answer, you have a potential lesson to teach. By probing with questions, you will uncover small deficiencies in their understanding. At that point, you can deliver a series of insights that fill the gaps (while making you look fantastic).

The Lesson Plan

Here's an example of a simple lesson plan outline:
1. Assess level of understanding
2. Subject areas
3. Learning objectives
4. New vocabulary and definitions
5. Content
6. Materials (visuals)
7. Lesson sequence (easiest to hardest)
    a. Beginning (introduction)
    b. Middle (methods and strategies)
    c. End (summary and understanding confirmation)

When you've finished, provide the lesson in a portable format. Make sure it's in a "to-go box" at the end of the meeting. This could be a thumb drive, a nicely printed copy of the material, or some other branded item that is tangible.

The beauty of a well-delivered lesson is that it leads to great insights that act like a Trojan horse. Once the prospect fully understands the insight, they will probably take it back to their company and teach it to their colleagues, managers, and bosses. It will make them look great, and it will help you close the business.

Just make sure that whatever lesson you teach points back to the primary benefit or result delivered by your product. This will elevate you to expert status and, again, enable you to charge more than lower-priced competition.

Cognitive Behavioral Therapy for Selling

In psychology, currently the most effective therapy to create long-lasting behavioral change is called *cognitive behavioral therapy*, or CBT. When we experience a trauma, we change our behavior in some way, usually for the worse. If we get into a car accident, we may avoid a specific route to work or we may stop driving altogether. I have a friend who won't fly on a certain aircraft because of a traumatic turbulent event. He will look at the model number on the open door of the plane. It's usually engraved on a metal plaque on the interior rim of the plane door. If it's the wrong model plane, he'll turn around, walk off the jetway, and rebook on a different plane.

The therapist helps by reframing the trauma using altered context, perspective, or reimagining the experience. The goal is to change the thoughts that elicit the emotions to reduce or eliminate the negative behaviors. In CBT, this is called *cognitive reframing*. For example, if you are like my friend and had a bad experience on a specific aircraft, the therapist might pull the statistics of that aircraft and show how few incidents there actually were and how the turbulence was not aircraft-specific. Essentially, it is a matter of changing your thoughts. Holding new, constructive thoughts reduces the emotions associated with the traumatic event and changes behavior.

You can use a variation of this approach to increase your sales. You can use the insights you develop in the same way as a psychotherapist does. By changing thoughts or increasing understanding, you can empower the buying behavior you seek.

Insights can work to change how someone sees your product or service and allow them to feel better about making a buying decision. The best possible combination is to combine an insight with a testimonial story, where the story is the lesson and the result is an understanding of the insight.

You can also use insights or combinations of information to provide context and perspective that your prospect can share. Let's say I'm a real estate agent attempting to sell a particular house. Prior to meeting a potential buyer, I might lay out my perspectives thus:

1. Interest rates are low.
2. Prices are only going higher.
3. This is the only house in this price range in the desired school district.
4. It is a single-story building.
5. The lot is large.
6. The trees on the property are mature.
7. The house has been recently remodeled.
8. The house has a pool and hot tub.

In this scenario, my job is to present and achieve agreement on five perspectives in a row. I would go down the list. Let's say I get to perspective two, and they disagree. The prospect says, "Actually, they are completing 100 additional homes of this size in this area, which should increase supply and reduce prices."

I would then use my other perspectives like this: "Yes, you're correct, but those additional homes will be two stories and on small lots, Does having a single-story home on a large lot appeal to you?"

"Yes, of course."

Then I would go into my next perspective: "Have I mentioned these trees are over seventy years old—the oldest in this neighborhood?"

Then I could move on to the next perspective. Once I get five agreements in a row, I would suggest that they make a competitive offer as soon as possible.

The goal of this perspective transfer process is to get the prospect to see the opportunity to buy the same way you do. Once they have agreed with you five or more times, they will be far more likely to make a buying decision or take the next action.

If your product or service is more complicated, you will need to create more perspectives. If you need to get agreement from different stakeholders, like business development, engineering, and human resources departments, you will need to create a collection of perspectives for each stakeholder.

This is an excellent exercise to conduct before any presentation where different interests and incentives will be represented.

12

Discovery: The Art of Listening

The discovery process could be called the listening process, because that's the goal of discovery. The more you can get your prospect to talk about their problems, pains, and challenges, the easier it will be to address those items in your presentation. Think of yourself as a business therapist, and create space and silence to let your prospect vent about their problems.

As mentioned earlier, the average person speaks at 150 words per minute but can think at 500 words per minute. To make sure you are engaging your full brain capacity, listen with a pad of paper and a pen, whether in person, in a virtual meeting, or over the phone. The smallest details usually become the most important reference points.

Clubs and Spears

There are two types of discovery questions: clubs and spears. Clubs are big blunt objects which represent big, open-ended questions.

They act as invitations for your prospect to talk in an unstructured way about what's on their minds, current problems, pains, and challenges.

The key to asking these questions is to resist the temptation to speak. If you do speak, make sure it's to ask for more details and elaborations. The goal is to have them speak for twenty minutes or more without interruption. During this time, you should be writing down as much as possible: names of colleagues; the history of the company; past problems, challenges, and pains; and attempted solutions.

At the end of this phase, repeat back to the prospect the key points you wrote down, and ask if you have a correct understanding. I've done this thousands of times, and more than half the time I have been corrected about some issue or point. This is a huge positive: if they correct your understanding, be prepared to throw some spears at that topic in the next phase.

Before any meeting, prepare three to five clubs and write them down so you don't forget or get carried away with small talk.

Examples of clubs are:
- How is your business?
- Why are we talking today?
- Can you tell me a little bit more about you and your business?
- What are some of the things you want me to address during our time together?
- I would love to learn more about your business. How do you think we can help?

Once twenty or thirty minutes have passed in this way, you can start to use your spears: targeted questions that focus on their specific needs. Your spears should be targeted by utilizing the information you learned from your clubs. The best place to start is with any issue they had to clarify because you couldn't articulate your own understanding.

Use your spears to get deep into the situation and to demonstrate how well you understand their situation or problem. Ask them to talk about the ideal solution, and take detailed notes. This is also a good time to probe for understanding. Ask some questions that expose their knowledge, and use that to plan your insight strategy.

The Agenda

Always show up with an agenda. It doesn't need to be a formal document; you can write one out thirty minutes before the meeting. It should contain the following elements:

- Time and date.
- Participants: decision makers.
- Topics and key points. Why are you meeting?
- Ask for additions.
- Set the expectations.
- Desired next step.

You should kick off the meeting. You asked for the appointment, confirmed it, and now you're getting their valuable time.

The agenda serves a dual purpose: it proves to them that you value their time, and it shows that you consider your time valuable as well. Here's the order of operations:

1. Introduce yourself: your role, your colleague's role, the company.
2. Do a roll call and ensure everyone is present. If your meeting is virtual, ask if you can record the meeting for reference.

3. Briefly explain the key topics or points you would like to address.
4. Ask if there is anything you missed. If there is, add it to the agenda. (This is also a huge positive, as it will laser-focus you on something you didn't know about before.)
5. Describe the end state in terms of what you want to accomplish and then ask for agreement. You can say something like, "Does that sounds good?" or "Is that OK with everyone?"
6. Lastly, state your goal in terms of the next step. Is it a trial, a purchase, another meeting, or a contract review? Whatever your next step is, state it out loud and then say, "If we do a good job, we would like to take the next step and [insert your next step]. Let's get started."

Step six is the most important step. A meeting without a solid next step is a waste of everyone's time. Never walk into a meeting without a solid, clear goal for a next step or a closed sale. The worst ending to any meeting is when people walk out and don't take any new action. When you state your goal upfront, the mindset of the meeting changes from information delivery to actionable opportunity.

13

Presentation: The Magic of Enthusiasm

BEFORE WE DISCUSS HOW to present with competence, charisma, and authority, we need something much more important than all those things: we need to demonstrate our belief through conviction. Let me tell you a story that I believe illustrates this concept perfectly.

Derrick and Verizon

As mentioned previously, I was promoted to the position of sales manager in my early twenties, which essentially meant that I was required to recruit, train, mentor, coach, and manage a sales team.

Building a sales team for residential door-to-door sales is a herculean task. You must recruit every day, cajoling, convincing, influencing. When you finally get someone into the office, that's when the real work begins.

At the time, the hiring process was as streamlined as it could be: a background check, a short application, and a twenty-four-hour waiting period. Once the applicant was approved, they were provided with a company polo shirt, badge, and clipboard. With these minimal armaments, the new sales recruit was given a day of training in the office, followed by a series of field training days with me or other experienced sales reps.

One day I was eating lunch at McDonald's, and a young man came walking up with a job application in his hand. I jumped up and intercepted him. I asked him if he was applying for a job, and he confirmed that he was. I then went into my recruiting spiel.

At the time we were contractors for Verizon, the large telecommunications company. We were essentially sales mercenaries hired because Verizon, with all its marketing might, could not convert customers to their new fiber-optic services. These services included Internet, TV, and phone service in a bundle that, when ordered together, would qualify the customer for a discount. Even with the billions the company spent on the infrastructure and the millions they spent on marketing, new and existing customers were not making the transition. So Verizon hired feet on the street to get the job done.

This young man was named Derrick. He had just graduated high school and drove an old white Jeep Wrangler. His hair was sun-bleached and a bit shaggy. He was on the shorter side and had a bouncy gait. I showed him my paycheck from the previous week and told him in a few short weeks he could be earning just as much (sometimes more, which was true). At the time, minimum wage for a full week of work (forty hours) was about $200. My paycheck was $2,200 for the week. He studied the paycheck for several seconds and then he agreed to meet me in the morning to apply for the job. We took him through the process. After a few short days, we gave him his own "turf," which is what we called a list of leads. It gave him three to five good-sized streets, or about fifty houses to visit.

In his first week, Derrick sold three deals, which netted him about $300. In each subsequent week, his sales got better. By week six, Derrick was selling five deals a day—an extraordinary feat by any measure. Here was a guy who had been about to apply at McDonald's for $200 a week. Six weeks later, he was making $3,000 per week. (In case you're doing the math, we worked six days a week.) I was astonished. I was the only other person in the office producing close to what Derrick was producing. I had to know what he was doing. What technique was he using? What was he saying?

I approached Derrick at the next office training and asked him if he wanted to conduct the next training in front of the team; we had about thirty sales reps at the time. He got visibly nervous and declined bashfully. I thought about it, then I made an alternative request: I asked Derrick if he would be willing to simply role-play with the other sales reps. He would stand in the front of the room and be presented with questions and objections that the other sales reps were receiving at the door. All he would need to do is answer the questions and objections just as he had been doing successfully.

He agreed, and at the next office training, he walked to the front of the room. We lined up all the sales reps in a single file line. Each one would approach Derrick and state one question or one objection they were struggling with. After about ten attempts, it became painfully clear that Derrick didn't know anything about the product and could not answer a single objection. How was this possible? How could he be closing five deals every day without any product knowledge or the ability to answer an objection?

I was embarrassed for him for a few minutes, but then I grew suspicious. What if this was fraud? What if Derrick was doing something dishonest? I became convinced that there was something nefarious going on, but I had no evidence.

Then I got an idea. After the failed role-play, I approached Derrick and asked him if we could knock on doors and sell together. I would not be selling; I would just be observing and taking notes. Derrick enthusiastically agreed: "Yah, totally. Let's do it!"

The next day, we met on his turf and started down the street. We got to the tenth house on the list, and a gentleman answered the door. Derrick jumped back, threw both hands high in the air, and with a jovial and emphatic voice said, "Hi, It's me, Derrick, with Verizon. How you doin' today, sir?"

The gentleman was taken aback. He paused and said, "No, no. I've looked into your service, and your prices are too high."

Derrick retorted even louder with a giant smile on his face, "Oh, but sir, we have the *best* prices! They're better than the prices you're paying now! They're the *best*!"

The gentleman responded, "OK, but you still don't have the football channels I want."

Derrick, waving his arms, almost dancing, said, "Oh, but sir, we have the *best* football channels. They're better than the football channels you have now. They're the *best*!"

The gentleman at the door took a step back, looked up in contemplation, and said, "OK, I'll take it."

I was totally shocked.

Derrick filled out the form, got the gentleman to sign, and closed the deal. I was surprised, but I concluded that every now and then you get lucky. Sometimes people are ready to buy; they just haven't gotten around to it yet.

We moved on. We went about ten more doors down the street. Derrick skipped up to the door of one house, knocked, and waited. We heard someone stomping through the house. After a brief silence, the door was thrown open. A woman glared at Derrick, looking upset and annoyed.

Derrick jumped back, threw his hands in the air, grinned from ear to ear, and raised his voice. "Hi, ma'am! It's me, Derrick from Verizon. How are you doin' today, ma'am?"

The woman, dead-faced and firm, stated, "I don't want your service."

Derrick threw both arms up high and with his whole body responded with bubbling positivity: "But ma'am, it's the *best* service. It's better than the service you have now. It's the *best!*"

The woman's face changed, contorted, and started to glow red with anger. She lurched forward with her finger pointing at Derrick's head as if she were going to shoot a laser beam at him. Then in a loud, angry voice, with spittle flying off her lips, she yelled, *"Look, bud, it's not a good time!"*

Derrick took a step back, immediately launched his body off the ground with both hands in the air, and countered, "But ma'am, it's the *best* time. There's no better time than now. It's the *best!*"

The woman looked a bit confused and began to scratch her chin. Some ten seconds passed, then she said, "OK, I'll take it."

Derrick filled out the paperwork, she signed the form, and he closed his second deal.

This went on for the remainder of his shift. Derrick closed five deals that day. I witnessed the whole thing.

I had to reflect on what I had witnessed. I had to rethink everything I thought I knew about selling. Here's a guy who knows nothing about the product. This guy can't answer a single objection, and he's outselling everyone else in the office. How could this be so? What strange dynamics were at play that I couldn't understand? What just happened? Could it be duplicated? The questions came in a flurry of confusion.

I knew what I saw, so I had to start there. If this is possible, *how* is it possible? What was happening inside the minds of the people who opened their doors? They were all originally put off and resistant to the idea of buying from Derrick. His pitch contained no significant information—no information at all. His answers to every objection were the same: "It's the *best*. It's better than what you have now." So it wasn't product knowledge or the ability to answer an objection. What converted these people from resistant skeptics to willing buyers?

My conclusion, as you may have guessed, was Derrick's overwhelming enthusiasm. Derrick was so enthusiastic that the people who encountered him at some point decided that they were not going to ruin his day.

Enthusiasm Makes It Easier

I wouldn't recommend that you attempt to sell on enthusiasm alone. But without it, everything will be more difficult. Without enthusiasm, you'll have to work harder and longer, and you won't like your work. With enthusiasm, everything will be easier. Things will magically go your way, and you'll accomplish more, earn more money, and enjoy your work.

Enthusiasm is the conduit through which conviction travels. I have used this one principle to generate millions of dollars in sales. It's real, and it works.

The secret to feeling the way you want to feel is to *act* the way you want to feel. The action precedes the feeling. If you want to feel motivated, act motivated. If you want to feel disciplined, act disciplined. If you want to feel enthusiastic, simply act enthusiastic. You have a doubt? Try it for yourself. You'll be surprised how fast it works.

Presentation Format

I have a wonderful business mentor that simplified the ultimate presentation format. He said, "Michael, tell them what you're going to tell them, then tell them, then tell them what you told them."

Simple, yet extremely effective.

When you tell them what you're going to tell them, you are building positive expectation. You're telling them the *what* and *why* of the presentation. In this key phase, resist the urge to tell them the who, *where, when,* or *how.*

You will also want to relieve the prospect of any tension associated with buying your product. Say something like: "It's our goal to show you that we can solve your problems in a way that's free, plus a profit. That is, if we *can't* show you that our product will save you money, reduce your costs, or increase your profits over time to the point that any investment you make will have a positive return, we won't sell you this solution. Our business is contingent on happy customers that love to give us referrals. If we're not confident that you will be happy and send us many referrals over the months and years ahead, we will not pursue a business relationship with you."

Clearly outline the reason you are presenting to them. Then summarize their current problems, challenges, or pains that you can solve, overcome, or relieve. Build more positive expectation by alluding to the solutions you are going to present.

Ask the prospect if your summary is accurate and complete. If it's not, ask them what they are most interested in. Listen intently—this is very important—and make sure you address any new points of interest.

Then tell the prospect the results you will deliver, in order of importance. Keep the list as small as possible. If your product has twenty-five features, the prospect will usually only want one or two of them. (You should have discovered these earlier in the sales process.) You can list all your features, but only present the one or two that have generated the most interest. Only elaborate on other features if specifically requested.

The next step is to show them how you will accomplish the results you previously stated: to "tell them." If you are solving multiple problems, address each problem individually. Define the specific problem, elaborate on the solution, then move on to the next problem in sequence.

During this time, you may want to request that questions be saved to the end of the presentation, especially if there are multiple stakeholders in the room. With several people, questions will lead to more questions and more tangents. It's important to stay on track. It's OK to confidently request that all the questions be saved to the end, as many questions will be answered during your presentation.

Remember, this is *your* meeting. Your job is to sell your product or service, not to allow your presentation to devolve into a brainstorming session. The group you are in front of work together, have frequent meetings, and are accustomed to a certain way of interacting. Be polite but firm: your time is also valuable. If there is only one or two people, then keep your presentation conversational; it should resemble a structured collaboration instead of formal presentation.

Many meetings are fun, interactive, and collaborative. Sales presentations are professional. The goal is to get a decision: yes or no (never maybe). Getting a no after a well-crafted presentation is OK. Nos are better than maybes. A no means "not right now." It's not a permanent state; it's likely an issue of timing. Commitments are difficult, require thought and accountability, and cost money. Act accordingly.

Once you've "told them," you can solicit questions, add clarifications, and show them other requested features.

Next, summarize by restating the problems and solutions: "tell them what you told them." Present three options, and ask them to choose what they would like to purchase.

Option 1: This option should be the lowest-priced one. It should contain 20 percent of the benefits or deliver 20 percent of the desired results. This is a great backup option if the prospect doesn't choose option two, because it makes them a customer. Current customers are ten times easier to sell or upsell to than new customers.

Option 2: This option should contain 80 percent of the benefits or deliver 80 percent of the desired results. It should be competitively priced but not cheap. It should be ten times more expensive than option one. This option should be at the apex of your bell curve. This is the option you want most of your customers to pick. It should be priced so that you or your company will be profitable with a reasonable margin.

Option 3: This option should contain 100 percent of the benefit or deliver 100 percent of the desired results. It delivers maximum service. It's the full red-carpet treatment: dedicated human and technological resources, priority access, top-shelf everything. This option should be ten times the price of option two.

You can tweak and iterate your own three options in terms of what they contain and what's included.

You offer these three options to give your prospect a choice of what to buy. People like to choose, even within the confines of a given range of options. They will enjoy reading through the list of what each option includes and selecting the most pragmatic one: option two. Option two will look like a great value in comparison to both option three and option one: maximum value for a reasonable price. You want to create a situation where if they don't choose option two or three, option one will seem like a low-risk way to try you out. Sometimes, they will choose option three, and that will be a big win for you and your company!

Mastering Your Physiology

On several occasions in my professional career, my brain wanted to do one thing and my body another. You can prepare thoroughly, practice in front of the mirror, gain confidence presenting over the phone or Zoom, but you can never fully prepare for the feeling of standing up in front of a large group or audience to conduct a presentation.

Two experiences stand out that will hopefully be instructive to you. The first was several years ago, I was selling software solutions for traditional publishers and broadcasters.

The solution I was presenting allowed traditional media to be more digitally interactive and connected. We used a series of QR codes, mobile phone short codes, landing pages, and payment mechanisms that allowed readers of newspaper and magazines to interact with hyperlinks embedded in QR codes. (This was before smartphones integrated this feature into their camera apps.)

I had worked tirelessly to get a meeting with Hearst Publishing, a large New York–based magazine publisher that owned *Marie Claire* magazine.

After months of going back and forth and following up, they finally agreed to take a meeting, which they scheduled in person. A week later I was off to New York City. I had thoroughly prepared for the meeting, and my team had provided me with a very compelling demo.

On the day of the presentation, I dressed in a suit and tie, polished my shoes, and ironed my shirt. All my boxes were checked: thoroughly prepared, with an excellent presentation, looked good, smelled good. Showtime!

I walked into the lobby and checked in. The Hearst Tower in New York is an extraordinary building. It cost $500 million to build and opened its doors in 2006. It was the first skyscraper to be built after 9/11. When you walk into the lobby, you are presented with three diagonal escalators taking people up and down. The escalators float on top of a large waterfall streaming water on all sides.

As I moved up on the escalator, I started feeling a little intimidated. I was a young man. I'd been to New York City a few times previously and only once before for business, which was for a series of small meetings with existing customers. This was going to be different.

I arrived on the forty-second floor, and the *Marie Claire* office split on the left and right between the print and digital departments. Our solution was somewhere in between, and both sides were curious about my presentation. I was greeted, and we started meandering through hallways that led to cubicles. I saw a small glass office with a few chairs set up. I assumed that was our destination, and I was relieved; then I was led past it. We turned a corner, and my guide opened the door to the largest boardroom I had ever seen: a long, white table with at least fifteen chairs on either side, with additional chairs lining both walls. There were already a dozen people casually chatting. I was guided to the front of the room with a large TV and some connectors for a computer.

As I started setting up, I started heating up. My heart rate accelerated, my palms got sweaty, and I could feel my head heat up and start to perspire. I had mentally prepared for a small meeting, not a big one. A nice young lady came over to inform me that the publisher was just wrapping up another meeting, and we were still waiting for the digital team to make their way over. She said I had some time if I wanted to use the restroom.

I walked out feeling anxious and experiencing an extreme fight-or-flight response. I made it to the restroom and looked in the mirror, and I was a total mess. There were beads of sweat on my forehead, and my hair was soaked on the sides and the back. I started taking long, slow, very deep breaths to reduce my heart rate. I removed my jacket, and my light-green dress shirt was soaked through. I dried my forehead, armpits, and chest, then I packed my armpits with several paper towels to absorb the sweat and put my suite jacket back on. I continued to breathe deeply.

I was running out of time. I remembered some advice I received about presentations: "It's not about you; it's about them. Everyone wants to have a positive experience. No one wants to go to a bad presentation." I calmed down a bit, dried off, and departed from the safety of the restroom.

When I walked back into the boardroom, I planted a warm smile on my face and acknowledged as many people as possible.

Everyone was there and sitting except for the publisher (the boss). As people continued to chat, I made some small talk with the people closest to me. As I familiarized myself with the people in the room, I became calmer and more relaxed.

Finally, the publisher walked in, very stylish and with confident swagger. She casually threw her stuff on the center of the table, sat down, and said, "OK, now we can start." She looked at me, smiled, and gave me an eyebrow flash, signaling my permission to begin. I started my presentation and maintained my composure. The attendees were engaged, and I was interrupted several times with positive affirmations about how this could work and be implemented quickly. The presentation was a huge success, and they agreed to a trial.

In hindsight, I imagine how the presentation would have gone if I had started as soon as I walked into the boardroom. That brief time in the bathroom saved me from what would have been a total disaster.

As I reflected on that experience, I realized that I needed to learn how to master my physiology. There's always a gap between what you think you can and what your body will let you do. Unfortunately, when you discover this gap, it's usually too late to avoid the negative fallout. Here are the valuable lessons I learned:

Wear a white shirt or a black shirt. If you sweat when you get nervous, these colors can save you. Do not wear light colors like gray, light green, light blue, or pink, as they will show sweat very distinctly. Also wear an undershirt that is not visible through your dress shirt.

Avoid drinking too much coffee on the morning of your presentation. You will have plenty of nervous energy you can use. Have some coffee or tea after your presentation, or after you begin your presentation if it's a long one.

Most important: breathe. Practice breathwork exercises far in advance of any presentation. The deeper and slower the breath, the faster the effects. Deep breathing is the only exercise that can reverse a fight-or-flight response. When this response occurs, your amygdala dumps adrenaline into your body, which is great if you're running away from an angry bear or swimming away from a shark, but super inconvenient before or during a presentation. The problem with adrenaline is that it shuts down your prefrontal cortex, which is responsible for your presentation skills, memory, rational thought, and ability to think creatively. The only way to wrestle control back from the amygdala is to breathe deeply into your belly and chest, hold your breath, and let it out very slowly. Repeat this process five times, each time exhaling more slowly.

Start with a familiar and well-practiced story. Tell an amusing but relevant story for the first five minutes of your presentation. All your physiological reactions will happen in the first five minutes. If you can get through a short story, you will set yourself up for a smooth presentation. Plus, people love stories. If you can, make them laugh. Laughter is wonderful medicine for nerves.

I had a boss and mentor who would start meetings with the same story. He would ask, "Do you know why I started this company?" (Pause.) "Because I got angry!" Then he would launch into all the reasons he got angry and why he wanted to solve his frustration by creating a new product or service. Everyone would be smiling and would be eagerly anticipating the remainder of the presentation.

Before the presentation, acknowledge that everyone wants you to succeed. They didn't take the meeting and allot the time so that you could come and fail. They have a positive expectation, they're curious, and they want to learn. If you tend to get into your own head—thinking about yourself and how you look or sound or doubting your competence—remember, it's not about you, it's about your audience. Focus on delivering the most value possible.

The Presentation: Key Visuals
SHOW THEM IT'S FREE

If you can, show your audience that your product or service is free.

Here's a simple visual you can use:

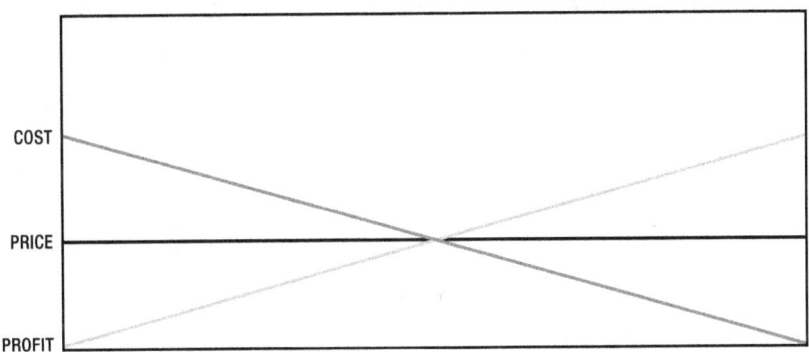

You can show the prospects that your product is free in multiple ways. The first way is to show them that by purchasing your product at your price (indicated by the PRICE line on the graph above), they will save money over time, making the cost of your solution zero at some point in the future. The second way is to show them they will be more profitable by using your solution (see PROFIT line). At some future point, their additional profits will exceed the price of your product, making it free. As more time passes, the cost savings and/or additional profits will continue to grow.

ELIMINATE THE RISK

Provide a 100 percent money-back guarantee for any reason. If you are confident that you can deliver value, providing a guarantee is a great way of eliminating risk. Few people will take advantage of this guarantee, especially if your business does a great job with delivery, customer service, follow-up, follow-through, and problem resolution. You can sell ten times more with a guarantee, and only a few people will ever use it.

Here is the other wonderful benefit of a guarantee: when someone feels they're not getting value from their purchase and they ask you for their money back, they are giving you an opportunity to save your reputation from negative word of mouth and bad reviews. One bad review can sabotage hundreds of potential sales.

SHOW YOUR TEAM

Do you work with a group of people? Take a picture of all of them with you included. Use this picture to humanize yourself and your company. Put that picture on your website and use it in your presentation materials.

From years of experience, I know that people can easily reject companies, products, and brands, but they can't easily reject people. As soon as someone sees your company photo, it will be much more difficult for them to treat your products or services with detachment. They will see all those smiling faces when they consider purchasing your products and services.

SHOW THEM YOUR CUSTOMERS

Have an image with a collection of company logos arranged in a mosaic or grid. Seeing your collection of logos is a powerful display of social proof. Resist the urge to make some logos bigger than the others: keep all of them the same size. This way, you're intimating that you treat all your customers, big and small, the same way. Put this image on your website, and include it in your presentation and closing materials.

YOUR PRODUCT, SERVICE, OR TEAM IN ACTION

Create a short video that demonstrates your product or service doing what it's supposed to be doing. If you sell weed whackers, show your weed whacker cutting through weeds like butter. If you sell a software program, create a sizzle reel showing all the features working together seamlessly. If you sell industrial food packaging equipment, show the production of 100 cans a minute with a peppy soundtrack. If you sell training services, show your trainers in front of a bunch of engaged and happy people.

You get the idea. Think of your product or service as a movie and create a trailer for it, showing all of its intriguing, compelling, and curiosity-evoking elements. This will prime you to have constructive and productive conversations with your prospects, and it will help them visualize using your product.

14

The Close

Now it's time to close the sale! You've completed all the hard work, and now it's time to funnel all your efforts into a single point: the close.

Unfortunately, it's not 1985, when a collection of boilerplate lines would somehow cause your prospect to say yes and sign on the dotted line. It's the twenty-first century, and closing the sale is less about wordsmithing and more about leveraging the trust you have developed. You've built trust to glean information about your prospect. You've used that information to identify real problems, pains, and challenges. You've taught and empowered them with industry-leading insights and positioned yourself as an expert. You've presented their problems back to them with your solutions. You've given them different options to buy your product or service, and now it's time to welcome a new customer to your business.

You need a plan: a closing plan.

The Three-Part Closing Plan

Over the years, I developed an effective three-part closing plan. You can prepare it in advance of your meeting and use it if you have a closing opportunity. You can also use this plan if you need to come back to close the sale.

Note that if you are ever asked to come back to close the sale, you should confirm an exact day and time to return before you leave. When you show up, don't expect the sale to fall in your lap. The enthusiasm and empowerment you built during your presentation is now gone. The prospects will be thinking only about the money, the commitment, and the obligation you represent.

You need show up with same level of enthusiasm and energy you had during your presentation. Be prepared to recap your entire presentation. As often happens, there may be new people who are curious and need to weigh in. Once everyone is informed and satisfied, you can use your three-part closing plan.

The first part of the plan is to summarize the prospect's problems, pains, and challenges. Reiterate the reason why you're there in the first place. Do it clearly and confidently.

The second part of the plan is to show the solution, relief, or strategy your product delivers and how it relates back to each problem, pain, and challenge.

Lastly, the third part is where you show them their buying options. Remind them which one they selected or gravitated to and ask them to confirm their choice.

Then, and only then, can you start your closing process using a tactic from the list below.

These are not closing strategies, simply crutches that you can use to feel more comfortable initiating the close:

The next step close. This simple and effective close should be your default. It's a very easy, low-pressure way to start the closing process. After you've presented and answered their questions, you give them a few buying options. Then you can say, "Now the next step is to choose the best option for you. Which option looks best?" or "The next step is for me to collect a deposit. What is your preferred payment method?" Whatever your next step is, you simply state it and then start the transaction.

The assumptive close. You assume the prospect has already agreed to buy your product or service and start your closing process. Start filling out the paperwork.

The pen to paper close. If you have an order form, ask them for their information and start filling out the form—phone number, address, and other information. If they give this to you, they're ready to buy. Or combine this with the next step close and ask, "The next step is to fill out the form. What address would you like us to put on file?" Or "What contact number is best for the delivery person?"

The invitational close. At the end of the presentation or conversation, you can ask them to give your product a try: "Why don't you give it a try?" or "How about giving our company a try?"

The future forward close. Ask about some future action, contact, or service. For example, you can ask who your point of contact will be moving forward, or when they would like to schedule their first service. If they answer as if they're already a customer, start your closing process.

Alternative choice or trial close. Ask the prospect to pick their favorite color or size, or have them select between two options. If they tell you their desired selection or pick an option, start your closing process.

Authorization close. If you have a service agreement or work order, you can give it to them and ask them to authorize it. You can say, "OK, if you'll just authorize this, we'll get started." With this close, be sure to stay silent while your prospect reads through the material. Stay calm and relaxed and resist the urge to speak first, even if the silence is awkward. If a question comes up, answer the question completely, then go back to silence. At this point, you're no longer selling: you're now giving them space to decide and commit to you.

The most common reason that sales don't happen is that the sales professional fails to ask a closing question. If you do not ask a closing question, the answer will always be no. If you do ask a closing question, you may get a yes!

In between a no and a yes is something very valuable: a real objection. You will not receive an authentic objection until you ask a closing question. This is when all the unspoken objections come out. There is no sale without some resistance. In a vacuum, nobody wants to decide, commit, or spend money. It's your job to use the closing questions to get all the objections on the table. Answer each objection, and then try to close again. Go back to your three-part closing plan and restate their problems, your solutions, and their preferred buying option. Ask them to buy in different ways until they have no more objections or questions.

15

Dealing with Objections

OBJECTIONS ARE QUESTIONS. SPECIFICALLY, objections are questions designed to delay, defer, or defuse a buying decision. Nobody ever defaults to making a decision unless they are required to. Nobody wants to make a commitment unless it's 100 percent necessary. And nobody wants to spend money if they can possibly avoid it.

Not wanting to decide, commit, or spend money is the root of most objections. The prospect will do this by asking any question they can think of to delay, defer, or defuse a decision to buy.

If your product or service delivers excess value, you should not shy away from these questions. Each question means your prospect is thinking about buying your product, but they're not 100 percent convinced. In this context, objections are good. Imagine not getting any objections: where would you take the conversation? Objections are signposts pointing at the holes in your presentation. I know consultants who get paid to analyze and poke holes in sales presentations. Your prospects do it for free when they object or ask questions at the end of your presentation. These are gifts you can use to make your presentation better next time.

Talking about the Price

"What's the price?" or "How much do you charge?" Never answer this question until you have a good understanding of your prospect, because it provides the prospect with no useful information. It's important to recognize this question as an objection. It usually happens at the beginning of the conversation when you're trying to get an appointment.

What would it matter if your product was $5, $500, or $5,000 if the prospect doesn't understand its value? If you answer this question, you will inevitably get a response like, "That's too much" or "It's too expensive." In the absence of understanding the value you offer, any price you offer will be too high. Avoid talking about the price by using one of these lines:

"Because I don't know anything about you or your business, I don't know what the price would be. Do you have time on Thursday at 11 a.m. so I can learn a bit more and provide you with a quote?"

"I'm not allowed to quote pricing until I learn more about you and your business. Do you have time on Thursday at 10 a.m. or 2 p.m. for a short meeting?"

Use the prospect's curiosity about the price to confirm the appointment. Whatever you do, in the beginning of any conversation, do not quote a price. The one exception is if you sell a commodity where price is the only differentiating factor: then you can offer a price upfront.

Price Objections

What happens if you get price objections at the end of your presentation? The prospect knows everything they need to know to make an informed decision, but they think your price is too high. This happens when you don't show enough value. In the graph below there are three bars: *cost*, *price*, and *value*.

The *cost* is how much your company spends to deliver their product or service. The *price* is how much you charge. The difference between price and cost is the profit and the range with which you have to negotiate. The *value* is how much benefit your customers receive for the price.

What would happen if the perceived value is less than the price? Your prospect will object and say the price is too high. What's the solution? Find a way to increase the perceived value to the customer or increase the value of the offer.

The worse alternative is to lower the price or give a discount. Price reduction and discounting are far worse than maximizing value, because this tactic reduces the profitability of your business and potentially decreases your commissions. Discounting also diminishes the prospects confidence that they're getting the best price. Instead, find creative ways to increase the perceived value of your product or service.

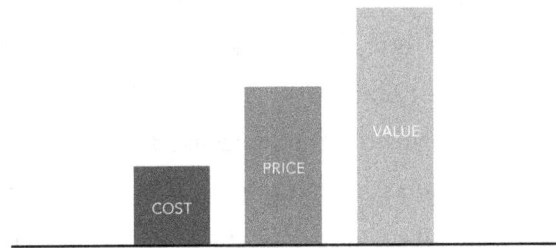

Timing Objections

Some people get paid once or twice a month; most businesses budget by the quarter. Consequently, timing is essential. If it's not the right time, that's OK. Unless you can offer some deferred payment plan or interest-free financing, it might be best to wait for a better time. Ask when they get paid and follow up then. Or ask about their budget planning process.

In the past, when I worked for a large bank, I learned that their process took nine months for expenditures to get approved. The bank would evaluate options in Q1, approve their chosen options in Q2, then fund those purchases in Q3. It didn't matter how skilled and savvy the salesperson was: there would be no potential sales for at least seven months. If it's a monster client, it will be worth the wait.

Evaluation Time

The dreaded "I want to think it over": this objection can be annoying, because it derails the conversation. You can't say, "No, you can't think it over." I mean, you can, but you will likely lose that sale.

There are two strategies you can use to address the above objection. The first strategy is to get out in front of it. At the beginning of the presentation, say something like this:

"In the interest of time, I will present to you all the information necessary for you to decide today. At the end of this presentation, I will ask you to buy this product, because I believe it will provide a preponderance of value, far more than its cost. My request to you is that you give me an unequivocal yes or no answer at the end of the presentation. Is that fair?"

With this line, you will change the dynamic. Everyone in the room will be truly evaluating your presentation with the goal of either buying or not buying. Your presentation will not devolve into a conversation or brainstorming session.

At the end, ask your unequivocal yes or no question and take the answer like a champion. If it's a no, thank everyone for their attendance and attention, pack up your stuff, and leave. Remember, a no often means that it's not the right time. Often, you will get a yes. What you will not get is a "we want to think it over."

The next strategy is simpler. Once you receive the "I want to think it over" objection, say, "Of course, that makes perfect sense. Is there any additional information I can provide to help with your evaluation?".

If there is, this is a perfect opportunity to follow up sooner than later. If not, pack up your stuff or conclude the meeting. Just before the meeting ends or you walk out of the room, ask, "Can I ask one last question?". Then ask, "Was it the price?"

This forces the prospect to admit that it is the price, and you can now address price concerns. If it's not the price, the prospect will tell you what the main objection is, and you can address that objection and try to close again. When you act as if the meeting is over, the prospect relaxes. They'll feel safe because they didn't buy anything. In this state of relaxation, they will be more open and honest with you.

If they're analytical buyers, give them as much time as they need to think it over. This is exactly how they like to buy. When you follow up with an analytical buyer, send them some data points, studies, graphs, or infographics that highlight the benefits of your product or service.

Your prospect's objections and your answers are like two sword fighters exchanging swings until they're both out of breath and exhausted. At some point, you will exhaust your prospect with all your thoughtful answers, and there will be silence. In this silence is the perfect time to ask a final closing question. The silence is created by the cognitive fatigue of your prospect, indicating that they can no longer think of any good objections. In this silence, they are telling you that they are ready to buy.

16

Multiple Sales and Referrals

As I've already pointed out, it's ten times more difficult to get a new customer than it is to sell to an existing customer. Yet most sales professionals will default to prospecting for new customers. Everyone needs a customer acquisition strategy, but not at the expense of the opportunities you can create with your existing customers. You should be incentivized to sell to both new and existing customers.

Many sales professionals think of a referral as a special bonus, an unpredictable reward, and then they go back to prospecting for new customers. Instead, a referral strategy should be active and intentional. Contact your existing customers on a regular basis. Add it to your CRM or calendar. Maybe dedicate a certain day each week to your referral strategy and contact only existing customers.

Every new customer should be treated as if they're going to be a customer for life. Begin with the end in mind. Ask, "What sort of experience would this customer need to have with my company for them to buy, buy again, and refer their friends?" Then resolve to treat them that way. The key is to delight your customers in fun and imaginative ways. Go above and beyond with customer service. Be proactive by discovering customer issues before they contact you.

Start thinking in terms of lifetime value. Each customer represents unimaginable opportunity. Every company that is doing well has a special focus on the lifetime value of their customers. How can you keep a customer over a long period of time? Or a lifetime? You transform them from a sale to a fan by moving through the seven phases below:

1. **Sale.** Someone buys from you for the first time. A first-time buyer will be the most skeptical. They will be suspicious of your product or service. They will be especially scrutinous of your customer service. This phase is the most important, since, as already noted, getting a new customer is ten times more difficult and expensive than keeping a customer happy. Make sure you have an after-sale plan that involves multiple touchpoints and some unexpected value. This could be as simple as a handwritten thank-you card. Other options might include a free sample or free trial of other products and services you offer.

2. **Multiple sales.** The customer buys from you again and again. Congratulations! The most difficult part is over. They are coming back and buying more. This is great confirmation that your business is operating the right way. Keep it up!

3. **Referral.** They buy from you and tell their friends and associates to buy from you. They also are willing to refer you to other friends and colleagues if you ask them. (You still need to prospect

for referrals. Getting referrals passively is a wonderful little bonus, but you still need a proactive referral strategy that involves contacting existing customers and asking them to refer others to your business.)

Here is one question you can ask that has to the potential to double and triple your referral sales: *are you happy?*

When calling existing customers, always start with this question before you ask them anything else. For example:

"Hi, it's Michael calling from XYZ company. I just wanted to check in with you. Are you currently happy with your experience with us so far?"

If the answer is yes, say, "Great! Hey, would you by chance know of anyone else that may be interested in a conversation with me?"

Pay special attention to the word choices in the line above. I used the words "would you by chance" instead of "do you," which reduces the intensity of the question. Notice also that I am only asking for a conversation, not a sale or a new customer.

If the customer does know someone, say, "Wonderful! Will you do me a huge favor and send a one-sentence email introduction? I'll take it from there."

That one-sentence introductory email will provide an unspoken testimonial, a reference, and social proof all at the same time. That's one powerful sentence.

4. **Testimonial.** The customer buys from you, tells everyone they know to buy from you, and goes on the record to vouch for your product or service, brand, and business. This is the first time they will vouch for you on record. They will put their positive experience in writing. You need to acknowledge the significance of this

act. It represents an extreme and timeless confidence in our business. You should be generous with your gratitude and expressions of appreciation.

5. **Reference.** All of the above, plus they are willing to spend their time speaking and verifying their positive experience with your prospective customers. This is an unpaid salesperson who requires a prompt to engage but nevertheless accomplishes the mission. They will take a phone call and return an email to help you sell your product or service. This is not a customer: this is a friend to you and everyone that works at your company.

6. **Advocate.** All of the above, plus they are inspired to take it upon themselves to find and sell others on your behalf. If someone is sitting within three feet of an advocate, and there is any reason to talk about your product, they will. At this point, they are not just happy; they are proud to be one of your customers. They feel in their heart that if they don't mention your product, they are doing a disservice to the people they encounter. This is a beautiful thing.

7. **Fan.** They love you and your product or service and want more than anything for you to succeed. They actively recruit customers and evangelize them about your products and services. They line up in front of your business days before you open or release a new product. They camp out; they meet like-minded people and immediately bond. Anything your company says is true; any product your company releases is the best on the market; anyone who disagrees is wrong.

At this level, a business no longer requires a proactive sales strategy. The product or brand sells itself. When was the last time someone called you up to sell you an iPhone or a Louis Vuitton bag? This is when your customers become your sales force. If you manage to get to this stage, you evolve from sales professional to customer experience manager. It's the same job, with a new title. You now can sell more at premium prices, and everyone is happier. In fact, they're delighted!

MVS: Minimum Viable Sale

In product development there is a methodology called MVP or *minimum viable product*. MVP works by only selling what people are willing to buy, one feature at a time. It is a customer-driven product development strategy. Instead of building what you think people want, you interview potential customers and let them choose the feature that is most important to them and they are willing to pay for. Then you develop and deliver that feature. Once the customer is happy, you can ask them what feature they would want next, then you develop the next feature, and so on. After this iterative process, you'll end up with a highly usable and desired product.

The corollary in sales is MVS or *minimum viable sale*. Your MVS is the smallest increment of your product or service you can sell. It's the lowest tier or smallest quantity. Even if it's not worth the time and effort upfront, it ensures that you at least get a new customer. Once you have a customer, you can upsell and side-sell more and bigger products and services. This is especially relevant for anyone that sells insurance, financial products, software, or food products.

For example, if an insurance agent sells someone car insurance, later they can sell the same customer life insurance, homeowners' insurance, umbrella policies, and even annuities. As the relationship grows, so does the suite of products used by the customer, and the customer becomes more entrenched with your company.

The Apple ecosystem is another great example. An iPhone is a gateway product to a Mac, iWatch, Apple Music, Apple TV+, iCloud, and other items. Each new product or service acts like gravity pulling the customer further into the ecosystem, making it difficult to switch to a competitor.

If you can't sell your desired offer, have an MVS in your back pocket. It should have a low price and be low-risk. Even better, offer an unconditional money-back guarantee for any reason. Win the prospect over as a customer, then grow the relationship over time. Again, it's ten times easier to upsell an existing customer than it is to get a new customer.

17

Gaming the Sale

MULTIPLE STUDIES HAVE PROVEN that status is a more significant motivator than money. I've personally seen this at work in multiple companies and sales offices. By assigning points to desired behaviors and rewarding the highest scorers with elevated status, you can drive your sales results to new heights.

In a sales context, you can reward salespeople for the number of outreach attempts, confirmed appointments, presentations delivered, or demonstrations made—any desired outcome. Display the top scorers using a scoreboard, and update it daily. You can use stats from your CRM to compile the data. If it's just you, you can play against yourself by comparing your performance to that of the previous day or week.

Select a reward before you start playing. It could be a big purchase that you can't currently justify, or, on a smaller scale, some sweet treat or time off. If you're on a team, it could be a preferred parking spot, free lunch, separate office, or preferred desk. One office had an especially comfortable chair that only the winner could use, like a throne.

Here are some other fun games that will help rewire how you think about sales activity.

A hundred contacts before noon. In this game, the rules are simple: whoever makes 100 contacts before noon gets a prize. Play this with yourself or as a team. Nobody ever gets to 100. They will inevitably get sucked into a conversation, appointment, or presentation, and they will likely sell something, which is better than any prize.

The "no" collector. It's like the previous game, except that the goal isn't activity; it's rejection. This game takes the sting out of being told no. Try to get ten rejections in two hours. You can play in the morning and the afternoon. Once you flip the script and make the negative outcome the goal, the positive outcomes are inevitable.

The board game. Think of the entire sales process as a board game:

Rules of the Game

The image on the opposite page provides a summary of the entire sales process, distilled into a board game. The pieces on this board game are your potential customers. The point of the game is to transform a lead into a fan by moving them through the process.

Your competition is every other company trying to get that customer. You're also competing with every other distraction the customer is faced with daily. Your reward for playing the game will be a higher income, a growing business, and more market share.

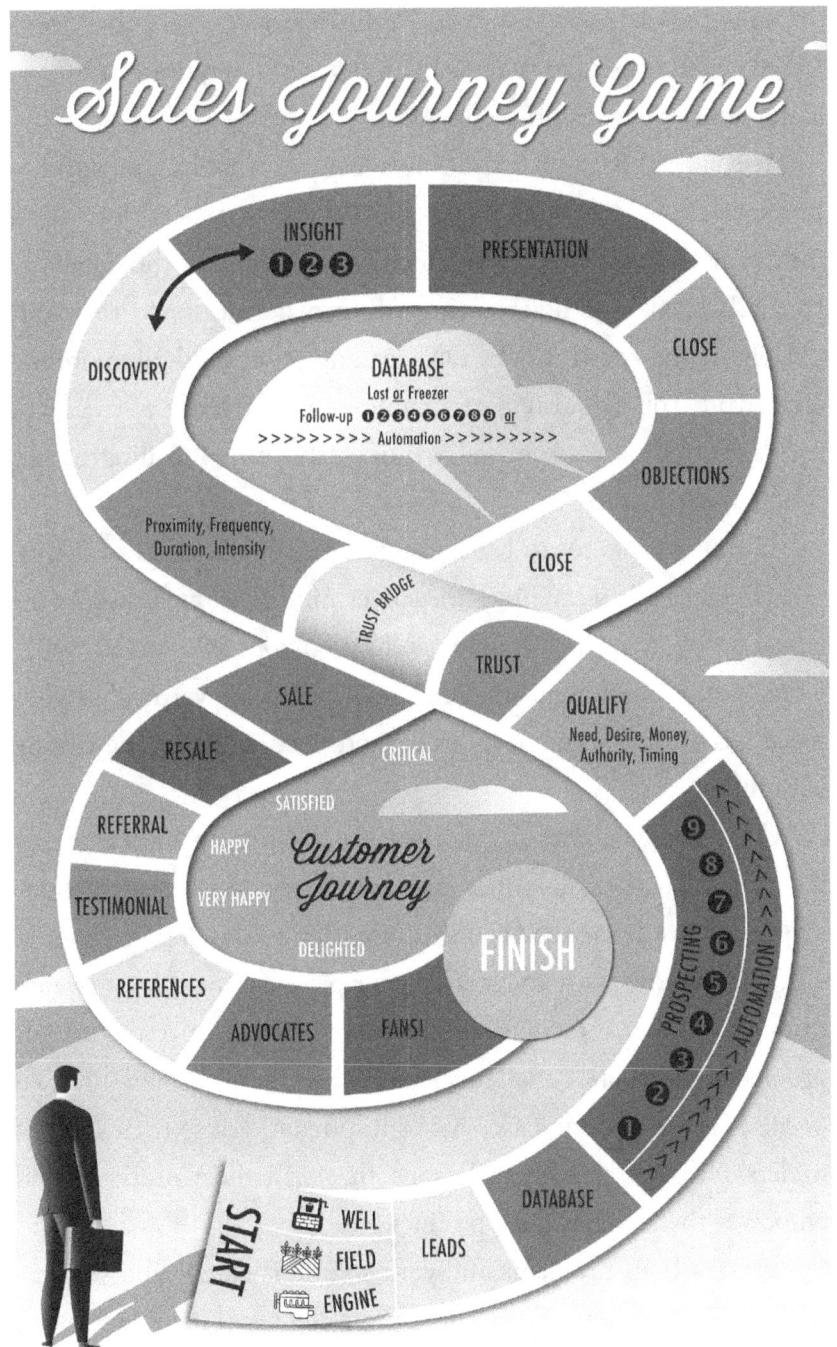

Imagine each lead you place on the board as a piece that needs to be moved over each square. Each move will require you to take action and exercise a different skill.

You start this game by finding a "piece"—that is, a prospect—in your well, field, or engine and entering their contact information into your CRM or database. Once your piece is in the database, you will need to contact them. You can decide to do this over the phone, by email, SMS, DM, or any other method appropriate to you. You can also start an automated sequence of emails or messages that have a specific goal of establishing meaningful and productive contact.

If you choose not to use automation, you will need to manually contact your piece nine times over nine to eighteen weeks (or adjust for more or less time depending on your sales cycle). Once a connection is established, your goal will be to verify that your piece has authority, money, desire, and need and that the timing is right.

Once the customer is qualified, establish trust by presenting your experience, testimonials, and references. If a better relationship is required, use the friendship formula to develop it.

You are now ready to listen to your prospect for at least twenty minutes without interrupting (see chapter 12). Learn about their problems, pains, and challenges and write the information down or log it into your database. Ask questions to assess their level of understanding; then select lessons that will most motivate and empower them to buy your product.

Present their problems and your solutions clearly and sequentially, making sure to show how your product will solve each issue. Demonstrate your product if necessary.

Give your piece three options to buy your product and ask them to choose the best one for them.

Explain the next step and move to close them with your three-part closing plan. Answer any last questions or objections. Try to close again.

If the timing is off, save the prospect by putting them back in your database with an automated follow-up sequence to ensure you are at the top of their mind when the timing is better. If they firmly reject your offer, put them in the freezer (long-term storage).

Once the piece agrees to buy, help them across the trust bridge. Make sure they get their product or get service right away. Ensure that your piece has a delightful experience throughout the entire game.

Move your piece up through the fan creation ladder. Each piece will need to be moved up with a different sunshine strategy (a strategy that provides delightful experiences for your customer).

The ladder's seven rungs have already been described above: sale, multiple sales, referral, testimonial, reference, advocate, and fan.

This game never ends. The better you get, the more money you make. Enjoy!

Conclusion

I HOPE THIS BOOK has inspired you to think better, be better, and take action in sales. Action is the best education. Learning new things allows us to know more, but true wisdom is only achieved through experience. The knowledge in this book is designed to give you the confidence to act. Through iteration and refinement, you'll get better and better. The best journeys contain a series of unexpected challenges, setbacks, and failures, but the hero always persists until they succeed.

Several years ago, when I was conducting sales training workshops all over the world, I started getting asked to do speaking engagements. They would say, "Michael, I can't take the team out of the field for a whole day. How about you come and speak for an hour or so?"

"Wow, I'm going to be a professional speaker!" I thought. I told my father, and he invited me to one of his speaking engagements. He told me he would introduce me to the organizer who might book me in the future. I joined the audience to watch my father speak.

Twenty minutes before the first break, my dad made an announcement. He said, "And today I've got some excellent news! My son Michael is here today, and he's going to come up to the stage and speak to you for next twenty minutes."

My father gestured for me to come and take the microphone. My heart dropped; I immediately felt the gaze of the 700 attendees. I stood up and walked to the stage. My feet seemed to be in the control of some other force. My hands started to sweat, and I could feel my heart pounding in my chest.

I took the mic and stared into the sea of people. The silence of anticipation was deafening. I stood silent, gaining control of my physiology, then I managed to tell a short story. I shared some good points on sales success, thanked the organizer, and concluded my performance. To my surprise, people applauded.

The big breakthrough was going through the sequential process of *knowledge*, *action*, and *experience*. Experience is the goal of life, knowledge is the prerequisite, and action is the catalyst. Once you have the experience, the fear dissipates.

This experience was a total game changer for me psychologically. I often think about that moment and reflect: if I had known in advance that it was going to happen, I would have made an excuse and tried to get out of it. Public speaking can be terrifying, but it's not the actual speaking part that's scary: it's the anticipation of doing something new.

As of this writing, I've spoken to over 100,000 people in sixteen different countries on topics such as sales, marketing, leadership, strategic planning, personal productivity, and time management. It's been an incredible and ongoing adventure. It is my goal that this book will inspire and motivate you to begin, or persist on, your own journey.

It's my hope for you that you will embrace your fears and move towards the actions that will cause them to dissipate. Fear and discomfort in professional life are signposts telling us where to go. Become a knowledge-to-experience translation machine.

It's time to put this book down and take action.

Your journey is just getting started.

About the Author

Michael Tracy is an entrepreneur, trainer, and speaker. He has started and sold businesses in marketing, legal technology, software, and professional training.

Michael has been teaching time-tested strategies and techniques for maximizing human potential for more than twenty years; first as a sales manager and trainer, then as a business owner and executive, and now as the Founder of Sales Journey, a business growth consulting company.

He has recruited, trained, managed, and motivated several sales forces that have achieved many millions in sales results, including a team that surpassed five thousand members. He has personally trained over 100,000 business owners, sales professionals, and entrepreneurs in sixteen countries.

Michael is also an entertaining, high-content, high-energy professional speaker. He teaches practical, proven strategies and techniques that people can use immediately to achieve their goals, increase their sales performance, increase their productivity and have better lives.

He is the co-author with his father, Brian Tracy, of the worldwide best-selling book, *Unlimited Sales Success*, now offered in twelve different languages and he also holds three issued patents from the USPTO for inventions in software technology.

Michael lives with his wonderful wife and three children in Cardiff-by-the-Sea, California.

www.ingramcontent.com/pod-product-compliance
Lightning Source LLC
Chambersburg PA
CBHW072154070526
44585CB00015B/1134